My Balkan Heart

A Voyage Beyond Culture, History and Empowerment

Mirjana Gligorevic

Publisher: Mirjana Gligorevic

Melbourne, Victoria

My Balkan Heart
A Voyage Beyond Culture, History and Empowerment
Mirjana Gligorevic
© 2021 Mirjana Gligorevic. All rights reserved.

Published by:
Mirjana Gligorevic
Melbourne, Victoria

All rights reserved. No part of this document may be reproduced or transmitted in any form or by any means, electronic, mechanical, photocopying, recording or otherwise, or by any information storage and retrieval system, without prior written permission of Mirjana Gligorevic (pronounced Mir-yana) or publisher (except by a reviewer, who may quote brief passages and/or show brief video clips in a review).

Image Acknowledgements: Ana Urošević, Jelena Šćekić, Karmela Marinčić, Ismet Islamović, Antonio Antonovski, Reddit, Orazio Fotti, Iina Kansonen, Rehema Miriam, Croatia Traveller, Ivona Antich, Roni Jackson- Kerr, Natalia & Jedrzej, Sean Peacock, Ej Wu, Ariana Kajic, Jovana Fuštić, Travelive, Shutterstock, Jeff Hartzog, Konoba "Orada", Duje Radović, EJ Wu and Mitar Milaković.

For permissions go to
Mirjana Gligorevic:
mirjanagligor@gmail.com
https://www.facebook.com/MGs-Adventure-Stories-105987178148742/

ISBN 978-0-6482336-2-6 (paperback)
ISBN 978-0-6482336-3-3 (eBook)

I dedicate this book to all who've had a tough life and feel stuck on their path, to people with a 'disability' or anyone else who feels like they're not living life to their full potential, and to passionate travellers who should explore the Balkan region.

> *"Until you spread your wings, you'll never know how far you can fly."*
>
> Napoleon
>
> https://quotefancy.com/quote/870127/Napoleon-Until-you-spread-your-wings-you-ll-have-no-idea-how-far-you-can-fly

Contents

Foreword vii
Back to Motherland 1
New Home 6
Greetings from Serbia! 9
Happiness Comes in Small Packages 16
At Baba Stoya's 20
Day Tour 29
Prime Hotel 37
Tour Sets Off 44
Niš, Skopje 54
Guided Tour in Skopje, Day 1 58
Guided Tour in Skopje, Day 2 62
Ohrid 70
Ohrid - Thessaloniki (sleep in Thessaloniki) 79
Thessaloniki - Delphi (Athens sleep) 81
Athens Attractions 86
Athens - Meteora 98
Meteora - Gjirokastra, Albania (overnight in Tirana) 109
Tirana 114
Tirana, Budva (sleep in Kotor) 120
Kotor 126
Tour of Dubrovnik 132
Split 142
Split, Mostar (sleep in Sarajevo) 148
Second Day in Sarajevo 160
Back at Baba Stoya's 174
National Museum of Serbia 181
Second Last Day 188
Last Day 192
Wonderland 201
Homecoming 207
Resources 211
Acknowledgements 217
About the Author: 219

Foreword

"Welcome into the world" is the most common phrase for many newborns, and the time of biggest joy for most parents.

My entry into the world eight weeks premature, and adapting during the first few stages of life, were very unpleasant in war-torn Bosnia. Surrounded by the noise of dropping bombs, my parents frolicked through a war zone with every visit to the hospital. Who knows if the uranium and other toxic environmental factors from war contributed to my life-long condition? After six weeks in an incubator I was released, so my parents thought my medical issues were finished and took me home. Up to this day, health consequences caused directly or indirectly by war keep taking a toll on many who've lived through it. Dad lost his parents at a young age, and his brother in war (prior to getting married), but he is the strongest man I know. I don't know how he's managed to sustain all that strength, but salute to him!!!

Just when the war started to settle down, my parents received the dreadful news about my Cerebral Palsy diagnosis. Like many parents would in that case, my parents asked themselves, *"why my child?"* I was only a baby then, so only time and growth could reveal the full severity of my condition.

We lived in a small city, almost on the border of Bosnia and Croatia, where everyone knew each other and the community gathering area was directly outside our building. With no awareness for people with a disability, I stood out for all the wrong reasons. To prevent my affected muscles from getting worse, I had to do a certain set of exercises every day, which I didn't enjoy. My parents were very strict on it and made sure I never skipped my daily homework. Even with a very mild physical disability, I had to undergo electro-galvanisation therapy followed by an application of hot smelly towels on my leg every few days. Immigrating to Australia in 2002, we were amongst the last families in line to leave the country due to the war. While it was a big relief for my parents, there were new challenges ahead for us all.

In Grade 3, I was eight years old and wore a prosthetic brace to soften my leg muscles. The brace wasn't very soft though, and sometimes caused me pain and woke me up at night. I went to one of the worst primary schools in Victoria. Apart from the fact I couldn't talk or understand the language, I was also known by the whole school as 'the girl with the plastic leg.' I was a typical loner who had no friends at school, and knew that more was out of place with me than just how I walked. In many cases, I would've preferred lunch time detentions over going outside. Sitting alone and watching other kids go down the slide at playtimes, while knowing I couldn't get up and over the last step, also made me feel like I missed out. When kids 'wanted to play with me' it was mostly tiggy, because they knew I couldn't run. I was bullied also, and because of this I changed schools many times.

Little did my parents know that Cerebral Palsy wasn't all there was to me. Half way through high school, it became official that I have Autism too. Girls on the spectrum are much harder to diagnose than boys, but I passed the assessment with flying colours. We can still achieve very much with the right tools and understanding though.

As a teenager, I had a big passion for tennis and competed with kids of higher abilities. I dreamed of competing in the Paralympics, but couldn't access the right resources. A lot of comorbid (one or more other conditions) factors come with autism, and I also had major depression, OCD and an anxiety disorder. When everything caught up with me, I dropped tennis altogether.

Like most people on the autism spectrum, I had my special interests, topics of passion, and liked gaining knowledge. While I had high stress and anxiety levels, I also had an intellectual capacity for some subjects, like most average and even some above average students would. However, most of my teachers overlooked it and just focused on how my anxiety would affect me and other students. They kept pushing me down to a special class at every chance, although I wanted to go to university.

MIRJANA GLIGOREVIC

I scored the highest on my English exam in Year 8, but was still switched to a 'special' English class in Year 10.

I was probably the least popular girl in my high school too—mostly I sat by myself, and I was left out of group work. I got bullied by the guy I used to like, and I missed out on a lot of experiences many other people got, such as birthday parties, going out with guys, night clubbing, the school formal and being a debutante. Knowing how many other girls would turn up to special events in high heels, while I wore sneakers with almost everything, upset me. I would've loved to be more girly and elegant too.

In Year 11 I discovered my passion for beauty therapy, but that went nowhere as the teacher treated me poorly in relation to my physical and social condition. On the last day of high school, every VCAL student got a card with the message, 'Congratulations on surviving 17 years of school' and they participated in the end of school march —except for me. I did not get the card and I was not invited to the end of school celebration march.

After finishing VCAL (a more practical program), I went on to T.A.F.E. and enrolled in Certificate IV in Tourism. At T.A.F.E. I learnt the harsh reality of how some people's minds never open with age, as I struggled with much older people in class who didn't want to look at or consider things outside their own point of view. I completed the general Certificate IV in Tourism, but didn't pass a compulsory unit of Certificate III in Retail Travel Sales twice, and the teacher kept emphasizing how I 'couldn't deal with business pressures' and I didn't meet the requirements for working in a travel agency. Not having a part-time job in my high school years has probably made it much harder for me to get a job later on too. While I enjoyed my volunteer work and felt a sense of helping the community, I was stuck out the back for six years with minimum interaction with people.

With a physical and a cognitive condition, I felt like one or the other always got in the way of some career path and struggled to find someone who'd give me a chance to reach my full potential. To keep pushing through those people who don't see potential in you is the hardest of all, but if you listened to each of them, you'd never get anywhere. Success and opportunities also depend on the type of people you come across in life.

After T.A.F.E, I came across a woman who had previously worked with someone on the spectrum. She had a great understanding of me and provided me with some work experience in her travel agency. She saw a great potential in me, but a family friend of hers took my place. People with my conditions can achieve just as much as anyone else in the right environment and with the right tools.

To this day, I'm still not sure if I went down the right path by not going to university, but more than just education, I value time and experiences.

Travel is a factor in living life to the fullest for me, that's why I wrote this book—to inspire others likewise.

In September 2019 I took part in the STEPtember walking challenge, with a goal of 5,000 steps per day to help raise funds for Cerebral Palsy initiatives. I completed 167,183 steps in total and raised $615.50. It saddens me sometimes, for those affected by Cerebral Palsy, when I see younger people who were born more premature than me and don't have a disability today, thanks to advanced medical technology.

Severe Cerebral Palsy often blocks the brain's pathway to basic body functions, and results in premature death too, yet is one of the least funded medical conditions. I learnt to ride a bike from a young age, something most people with Cerebral Palsy can't do. It probably comes as second nature to most parents of a child with a 'disability' to be more protective of that child. My parents were more protective of me when I expressed the desire to learn how to drive a car after Year 12 than they were when I was learning to ride a bike, but I got my license eventually.

I might've entered 'my first and only romantic relationship' in 2019, which was terrible and required professional intervention. One of the biggest misconceptions about people on the spectrum is that they're always happy on their own. From the age of twenty-five, witnessing how relationships, marriage and kids moved ahead for my generation and younger, while knowing that I haven't been out on any dates, became painful. Over time, I started to experience disenfranchised grief for myself (the unacknowledgeable one by others).

I hope I can make up for some of my missed experiences by travelling to authentic places. I discovered my passion for travel at eighteen years of age and started travelling at twenty-three.

As my parents witnessed my growth with age and how passionate I was, they decided that it couldn't just be all about their feelings anymore. They let me go free!

Knowing I was going to a place where I knew the people and culture probably made it easier for them too.

In 2018 I travelled solo through most of the Balkan countries, and now I write to share the beauty I discovered and my travel tips with you. Despite the war that separated us, in every country I felt the oneness that remains between us, and my connection with my heritage remains. I am trying to raise awareness about the less-known things that affect my people in the Balkans today, things I witnessed during my tour.

When a country has war, it can almost never go back to how it was before. (Germany and Austria are probably the only countries in history that rose back up after war.)

By travelling 'off the beaten path' you contribute to helping the country's economy too. My family were one of the lucky ones with the opportunity to emigrate for a better life elsewhere after the war, but many people left over there aren't as fortunate, so I'm glad that I started with bringing in the tourism $$ to my homeland first.

One thing close to my heart is the declining population of Serbia due to the number of people going out of country, and the question of how well we can maintain our values and history.

I'm dedicating my book to people with a disability who have a passion for travel, as well as people who like travelling in general and want to explore the Balkan region. Whatever your circumstances, I hope my story can help set you off on your own path, feel satisfied, and reach your full potential.

> *"You know it's time to take off as soon as you get the itch. You will have no choice but to take some steps alone in life to get to where you want to be."*
>
> Mirjana

Some people won't foresee your purpose, but you'll have your intuition and you can be your own best friend. At the end of the day, you can only count on yourself. The power that has sustained you all along won't leave you when you need it most. A friend who had severe depression successfully travelled solo to the other side of the world, where she lived for a year or two before I took off. She said the change of air and environment was a great refresher for her. She became my idol, someone I looked up to and my source of motivation.

I said to myself, "If she can do it, I can too."

Wings of encouragement get us much further than most people think.

Mirjana
(pronounced Mir-yana)

> *"Maybe who we are isn't so much about what we do, but rather what we're capable of when we least expect it."*
>
> Jodi Picoult
> https://www.goodreads.com/quotes/28842-maybe-who-we-are-isn-t-so-much-about-what-we?page=4

MIRJANA GLIGOREVIC

Back to Motherland

When you have a 'disability' you have to be extraordinary to be ordinary. I aspire to inspire—despite the fact I've been underrated my whole life.

If you finish university but still live with your parents, you're likely one of those people who save all your money to buy a house or travel the world. I was never very materialistic, but I knew there was something special about travelling. Wanderlust doesn't discriminate!

It just felt right to start my travel journey in my homeland, a place I can speak and understand the language. I'm originally from Bosnia, but came to Australia with my family in 2002 when I was seven-and-a-half years old. My grandpa passed away while re-building a future home for us when we were about to leave for Australia. I still keep some nice memories of us from back home (my godparents are still there). My parents put their heart and soul into learning the English language and settling well in Australia when they first arrived, but I think it comes as second nature to still have a connection with your motherland and origin, especially when you emigrated because of war.

I had to go back to see my country! We'd planned to go together as a family just before the Balkans flooded in 2014, then we had some financial insecurities the following year. I figure there'll probably always be something to potentially get in the way of what you want to achieve, but you have to find a way to make it happen.

Finally, in 2018, at age twenty-three, I decided enough holding back and that I would go solo this time! Sometimes you have to take a leap of faith, it's now or never!

> *"She travelled without waiting on others, and lived happily ever after."*
> Callie (The Lone Travel Girl)
> https://thelonetravelgirl.com/products/solo-traveler-mug

> *"If you want to fly, give-up everything that weighs you down."*
> Mirjana

Your first solo travel can be very daunting, but going to a country where you can speak the language and understand local culture makes it a lot easier.

Every accomplishment begins with the decision to start. Have you heard the saying, "The first step is always the hardest"? Sometimes it's just about getting your foot in the door. The moment I said goodbye to Dad and got into the 'passenger only' zone at Melbourne Airport I felt my first turning point.

I was struggling to push my day-luggage all the way into the plane's overhead luggage cabins due to a slight restriction in my left hand. After a few unsuccessful attempts at placing it right, somebody came and did it for me.

I think when you're consistently trying and not succeeding at a physical task in public, it is second nature for someone to come and help you with it, or ask, "Do you need help?" I usually ask someone to take my big luggage off the baggage carousel at the airport when I arrive too. There is also a button for calling flight attendants when you need them.

On the plane, I was sitting next to a flight attendant who was travelling aside from work. The tables had turned—the one who usually served people on a plane was sitting in the traveler's chair this time, and even got a photo of Uluru from her chair as we flew over. The feeling of being so high up above everyone else and 'no turning back' was definitely out of my comfort zone, but not as scary as some might think.

It's interesting the flight attendant didn't choose a business class seat, although she would've probably gotten a great discount compared to the other travellers.

Don't get rich, live rich. I have read a few articles about how people who became rich claimed money was their last sense of fulfillment when their life was ending. There are some things you can only learn by travelling this big world.

> *"When you're following your inner voice, doors tend to eventually open for you, even if they mostly slam at first."*
>
> Kelly Cutrone
> https://www.goodreads.com/quotes/390967-when-you-re-following-your-inner-voice-doors-tend-to-eventually

The flight attendant and I spoke about the away-from-home lifestyle and whether it impedes relationships. She was twenty-eight and met her current boyfriend at twenty-six. When you come across people who've been on a similar pathway to you but still ended with a positive outcome, it gives you a higher degree of hope. Her story gave me optimism that I can find the man of my dreams too.

By the time I reached Abu Dhabi, the weather had already gone from cold to hot. It was a big, eight-hour layover that started at midnight. What was I to do with all that time? I looked for a place to get some sleep, wondering if $250 was worth paying for a few hours of hotel sleep. Instead, I went to see if I could find any sleep lounges.

The airport workers directed me, but I still couldn't find it. My next question: When I found somewhere to sleep, should I grab something to eat or go straight to sleep?

The airport was huge! I felt lost, and kept walking between terminals one and three. I asked a few airport workers and they gave me basic instructions (left, right, etc.), but I still didn't spot it. I had gone back and forth a few times when a Bedouin man from the service desk, dressed in a long white shawl and dress, stopped me.

"What are you doing?" He obviously saw I looked lost, so asked for my ticket and recruited another airport worker to help me out. It was a quiet Tuesday night, so the other man took me straight to the business class lounge. He showed me what I was getting (the sleep and eat sign). The room was pretty much empty and had lots of food and sofas. I didn't know whether to feel bad or say thank you, but the man smiled and told me to, "be happy."

> *"You can't cross the sea merely by standing and staring at the water."*
>
> Rabindranath Tagore
> https://www.brainyquote.com/quotes/rabindranath_tagore_383735

My symptoms of Cerebral Palsy differ from time to time, but I think I'm more likely to get a limp when I'm exhausted. The next morning, an airport co-worker told me it would be a long walk to my plane and suggested taking me in a wheelchair. One advantage of having a visible disability is that people are more drawn to help you when they see it. It is important to know your rights and options when you have a condition, in this case, help with airport transfers. It's also important to trust the locals where you are—unless they seem dangerous.

On my final flight before landing in Serbia, I sat next to a friendly Indian couple from a less-known place. I got to meet them and enjoy a bit of a talk, while they opened up about their home and people from there. Just a little taste of culture and locals like this can be enough to open up your desire to explore a certain place.

They were going to travel from Serbia to Bulgaria, so I advised them to see Serbia when they got a chance. Although Serbian people are sometimes stereotyped based on their war-torn history, they're accomplished in putting it behind them and treating all tourists equally. I had chosen the seat by the window so I could get a nice view of my country from the air. A lot of travelers also say the wing seat is good for low turbulence levels.

Sadly, my phone batteries went flat in the last half hour of the flight. I felt a bit jealous of the girl sitting in front, who turned around and captured the whole landing view on her phone.

MIRJANA GLIGOREVIC

> *"Let your phone die and charge your soul once in a while."*
>
> — Mirjana

> **Travel Tip:**
> Remember to enter and exit at the front of the plane if you find the stairs difficult.

Serbia

New Home

The moment I landed in Serbia, I felt back at home. Stepping out of the checkout zone, the long-lost feeling of being in my own heritage came back to me like it had been there forever. Even if you were born in a different country, when you visit your motherland you might find the feeling of being at home comes up soon and the language sinks back in fast. How human genes work in this way is amazing! Before you know it, the feeling of being in your own place comes back, at least it did for me.

Uncle Mick and Auntie Lila greeted me and took hold of my luggage. Auntie Lila said the last time she saw my dad was at a wedding thirty years ago, but she said it in a way like she hadn't lost connection with him ever since. Uncle Mick is a flamboyant Serb with a local, authentic sense of humour. Driving to my new home in his rustic car gave me my first taste of the 'standard' living conditions of people in Serbia. His car had rattles and the odd shake, but everything seemed to work.

In Serbia I stayed with two cousins, Maya and Jenny, who live with their grandma, Baba Stoya, in a suburb called Apple's Landing, a forty-minute drive from Belgrade. After finishing high school in Bosnia, their parents supported them to move closer to Belgrade for better educational opportunities. Baba Stoya hadn't met me before, but she remembered my dad. He was the best man at her daughter's wedding, so she knew there was a bit of a connection.

My plan was to really experience my country again by arriving at their place three days before beginning my travels, and finishing my discoveries by spending three days with them after the Balkan tour.

Being in my own country where I understood the language and culture was a big advantage, but knowing I would be travelling with a professional guide on my first solo trip gave me great peace of mind. The guide notifies you of any differences in local rules before you arrive at a place, has a duty of care towards you (if you notify them of your condition prior), and can give you a better insight into some attractions. Even at home, I felt like I picked up a lot more information and hidden gems with a tour guide than I would have noticed otherwise.

> *"Having a place to go is home, having someone to love is family, and having both is a blessing."*
> https://tinybuddha.com/wisdom-quotes/somewhere-go-home-someone-love-family-blessing/

Saudade:
A nostalgic longing to be near again to something or someone that is distant, or that has been loved and then lost, "the love that remains."

The residential building I stayed in looked very old and unappealing from the outside, but never judge a book by its cover. Touring Baba Stoya's small flat brought back the yearning feeling, the opposite of nostalgia, if there's a word for the feeling of having returned to the place and time that was once significant for me, and took me back to my early childhood. It felt like a missing part of me was fulfilled.

The flat was only about forty-five squares, but had all the necessities to make the house a home in the most charming way. They had a mini oil heater, but there was lots of firewood out the back for when it snowed. The heat and smell of the original source of warmth is part of what makes the house a home.

Sofas were stretched into night beds when we went to sleep, then made again the next day. Some of these 'old fashioned' things are hard to beat.

My New Home

Staying over with cousins can be beneficial, especially for people on the autism spectrum.

To find out how visit:
https://mumcentral.com.au/cousins-connectionfami-
lyties/?fbclid=IwAR2Ue2OQUM7lHrplIigmIfHNVp9O3yt6jAqATDtYizlr
A_BOFCdQ_IOysPA

Day 1

Greetings from Serbia!

18 August 2018.
Greetings from Serbia! I couldn't remember the last time I woke up to the sound of a singing rooster! That was a new experience! So was Slatko.

Receiving a knock on the door from the milk man in the morning is a great start to the day for most mothers and grandmothers. We started each morning with a spoon of Slatko, even before breakfast, for a sweet start to the day. Slatko is a cultural treat, also known as a fruit jam. Housewives often make it from the fruit they harvest in season and store it in a jar with the delicacy of the original fruit in the centre. The first in line are cherries, wild strawberries and currants, followed by apricots, peaches, plums and quinces, then figs, watermelon and oranges, so says Marina Lukic Cvetic (Art Historian and Director of Study for Cultural Development).

https://www.facebook.com/Meet.the.Serbs/photos/a.101 50460039364968/10159953271804968/

The idea originated in Kraljevo as part of a Traditional Saint Day, but has spread over time and become more regular in many Serbian households. The key to happiness might just lie in these little things, or with a good start to the day.

"Start each day in a happy way..."
Mirjana

The plates and cutlery were smaller than you'd see in Australia, but the cute patterns on them added warmth to the home. I poured yoghurt from a carton with 'Moja Kravica' (my little cow) brand label and drank it from a cup. It was different and tasted better than ours in Australia.

Belgrade is a city where people put effort into their appearance. For the first time in ages, I wore make-up. The girls, who have a habit of putting it on, did a nice job for me, and I learnt that blush looks particularly good on me because I have light skin. It's a tip I can apply to future special occasions. When you don't put on make-up, just a little is enough to make you feel refreshed. We were visiting Tito's House of Flowers that day, so I put on a floral top.

Many who've travelled to Sarajevo say it is Europe's most underrated capital, but I beg to differ and say that it's Belgrade. (A majority of those travellers haven't been to Belgrade, which is less promoted or talked about).

As the bus reached the Belgrade CBD, Maya pointed to the site of the bombings from the 1990's wars. We wanted a photo in front of the statue of Prince Michael on a horse and asked a person to take it for us. The monument, sculpted by Enrico Pazzi, has stood at Belgrade Square since 1882 at the site where the Stambol Gate stood before it's demolition during liberation from the Ottoman Empire. There's some Italian influence behind it, and I find it interesting how a lot of European leaders are on a horse on their famous statues.

After Pazzi left Serbia, he wrote a beautiful letter:

> *"With a touched heart I leave this small town, the lovely center of this young but knightly kingdom, sister of my country. I have an Italian soul and feeling and in my heart I'm a delighted Serb."*
>
> Enrico Pazzi
> https://www.facebook.com/Meet.the.Serbs/photos/a.101 50982828889968/10152460986424968

The guy who took the photo didn't reply at first, because he didn't understand Serbian. We discovered he was an American who'd come to Belgrade to promote his music band. Two other guys with him were also American, and one was from

Argentina. We had a bit of a talk in English. It was the first time I heard my cousin speak English, and she impressed me with how excellently she spoke for someone who's never been to an English-speaking country. Many well-educated people have some knowledge of English. It's funny how sometimes we go back to motherland to experience our culture, while the locals there want to practice their English skills with us.

When travellers from that part of the world say they're going to Serbia, a common response from their locals is, "Why Serbia?"

"Because it looks cool..." (some said). I didn't expect many Americans would put Serbia on their travel list either, not after the media barrage with so much propaganda from America and the entire world about war crimes since the 90s, so meeting them in Belgrade was a nice surprise for me.

You might think the Serbian locals would frown upon some Western tourists when they come to Serbia, but it's actually the opposite. While many Serbs know about double standards for them from the majority of the world, they are also very welcoming and appreciate the people who come to see the real country and its people for who they are.

The music band originally planned to stay in Serbia for five days, but extended their stay to nine. They were probably examples of travellers who got a positive cultural shock, as I believe many from that side of the world would. After talking to lots of people, you would probably also gather it's much easier for others to adapt during their travel to Serbia, than for Serbian locals travelling overseas to adapt to some Western countries and cultures.

Anyway, the music band was going to Bosnia the next day and asked us where they could visit and where to promote their music. We mentioned Mostar and Sarajevo, but I forgot to mention Banja Luka, which has a Gospodska (Gentlemanly) street where a lot of interesting things happen.

> *"To travel is to discover that everyone is wrong about other countries..."*
>
> Aldous Huxley
> https://quotepals.com/2019/06/aldous-huxley-to-travel-is-to-discover

MY BALKAN HEART

Tito's House of Flowers was my first major attraction in Belgrade. It was a lot of stairs to get up, but it was nothing compared to what awaited me in Greece!

Josip Broz Tito was a very well-known leader during the time of communist Yugoslavia (half Slovene/half Croat), and successfully united the former Yugoslav countries post WW2. Some historians say all people from Former Yugoslavia (Bosnia, Serbia [including Kosovo], Montenegro, North Macedonia and Slovenia) share the same ancestors, and that is why post WW2 settlements declared us as one (Socialist Federal Republic of Yugoslavia) with Tito's Partisan movement.

How we technically speak the same language, with just a few different words, and have many last names ending with 'ic' is a good indication that it could be fact, although it's hard to believe it today, since the politicians have made so many divisions amongst us and many citizens fell under their influence.

There's a funny phrase on one of the united social media pages, "Ako smo u tuđini naši, zašto smo na Balkanu njihovi?" ("If we're our own in a foreign place, then why are we foreigners Balkans?")

The troubles between the constituent states date back to WW1, and you've probably heard stories in the media about the conflicts that took place amongst the Former Yugoslavia nations in the 90s. Many people say Tito was the only one who could've successfully united us. Some say if Yugoslavia still existed under Tito's communist system today it would be one of the most powerful countries in the world, and that's one theory about why the US launched an attack on Serbia, who was last to recognize the independence of the former country.

The way my cousin sees it is, "If former Yugoslavia didn't succeed in uniting under the monarchy there's no point in trying to unite it again. Like Luther Martin King said though, 'We must learn to live together as bothers or perish together as fools' ." Then comes the question: If Tito was so successful in uniting the country, why did everything start falling apart right after his death? Understanding this controversy motivated me to visit his place.

Inside the museum we met a Bosnian from Canada, who looked Asian. I borrowed his Partizan cap and flowers to make a good photo at Tito's gravesite. We went past many of Tito's trophies, which other leaders used to carry on days of his significance.

Unlike many leaders today, Tito built an alliance with the Western and Eastern parts of the world. When I saw the world map of how many other countries took part in Tito's funeral (209 delegates from 127 countries, including Australia and New Zealand), I realised just how loved and appreciated he was by the majority of the world.

I remembered seeing a link which mentioned that the Former Croatian War president used to be a member of Tito's Communist Party and achieved his goal of creating an Independent State of Croatia soon after Tito's death. We approached the security guy inside the museum with a question: Did Tito have anything to do with the ex-Croatian war president? I said if we had a guide I would've asked him, but he's probably now the next person available to ask.

Maya laughed at my inquisitiveness, and the security guy smiled too. She said such questions aren't of any interest to people in Serbia, and I think it might've been a surprising and humiliating moment for them. The security officer said he didn't know the answer to my question, but knew the former Croatian president went to jail for some reason. I suspect it was an uncomfortable topic that wasn't often broached, but they understood me as someone who came from the other side of the world and smiled in response to my openness and interest.

When you're a foreign tourist in Serbia, people also tend to be a bit more forgiving. I know many foreigners still find it hard to differentiate between the Serbians, Croatians and Bosnians when most of our surnames end with 'ic.' One particular Japanese tourist wore a Croatian t-shirt during his visit to Belgrade in 2018. He was convinced he was 'wearing the right shirt in the right country' and became the main attraction for tourists and locals. (That's not to say you should go to Serbia wearing a Croatian shirt though.)

Tito's Gift Museum next door was full of gifts from people all over the world. Tito often travelled the world to help people in less fortunate places and the people of Africa

MY BALKAN HEART

particularly loved him while Apartheid was still active. That also left him with less capacity for the people of his own country. Tito often used financial credit from other countries to provide the needy with free services, which contributed to the big debt and some economic problems in Former Yugoslavia (FY) post Tito. Whatever path you go down, especially in politics, there will always be complications with the good. That's why I really appreciate open-minded people and deep thinkers.

Although Yugoslavia doesn't exist today, I still found the old FY flag in peace at the museum. Another thing we didn't expect was to see a Chetnik badge on offer, in a place that supported Tito and his communist system. I definitely didn't expect to meet any of Tito's close alliances, but I did on my way out. The political professor had worked closely with Tito, and it almost felt like I met with the real Tito. It was so great to meet someone still alive from that generation. I bought a book he wrote on how Tito united Ex-Yugoslavia. Even if I don't read about politics, it was still very nice to have an item with his signature on it.

As we were walking back to have our lunch, we made our way through some street market stalls, stopping at one who was also selling historic badges. One caught my cousin's attention. It was a symbol which represented power and strength in WW2 for our people (similar to the rising of the sun). It looked Jewish, and we learnt we had some common ground with them. Serbs became for Croats what Jews were for Germans. Nazi ideologue Mile Budak led a regime to kill one third of Serbs in Croatia, convert one-third to Roman Catholicism and send the final third to exile.

The Serbs, Jews and Romans were held in the same concentration camp in Jasenovac, Croatia. Many Serbs suffered tremendously, but the Croatian fascists went a step further by putting the children in a separate concentration camp. Israeli historian Gideon Greif, who specializes in the history of the Holocaust, wrote a book in 2018 called *Jasenovac - Auschwitz of the Balkans*. These articles and resources usually come out on social media during the anniversary of the Holocaust, but the press articles often claim Croatians were the victims, when really, the Serbians were.

MIRJANA GLIGOREVIC

Have a look at:
http://hr.n1info.co/7NEWSMackay/m/English/NEWS/a478559/Croatian-government-commemorates-Holocaust-Remembrance-Day.html?fbclid=IwAR3cVuGXUFZcF049iHybJUxXcg9IEgvGLHlVtuo1-Oui7GNpeyvADVzB974

I hope that the movie *Dara of Jasenovac* which tells the true story will reach around the world and come to Australia soon.

My cousin thanked the stall holder for new knowledge, and we said we might see him again. It was a very warm Serbian goodbye with, "all the best," (svako dobro) from him.

Day 2

Happiness Comes in Small Packages

Baba Stoya showed me showed me her vegetable garden, Medo the dog, and the local community. Tomatoes and pumpkins are some of the most common vegetables growing in the veggie patches.

Starting your own veggie patch, chopping wood and lighting a fire are some skills that people in some of the other parts of the world never learn. Many elderly people from the Balkans who emigrated to countries like Australia don't like to look back because it reminds them of poverty, but I found it a beauty to see. Most of them have a veggie patch in their Australian back yard too though.

There is an element of happiness in picking from your garden and consuming your own homegrown food. Many families struggle financially, but zucchini is one thing they never run short on. Eating organic isn't a trend, but an ongoing part of tradition in some countries. When you stick to tradition, things don't lose value.

Some traditional Serbian homes also have a vineyard with an overhead grape arbor. The natural pergola blooms in season and the green leaves over your head provide perfect shade and cool during summer months. In early childhood, I enjoyed visiting friends and swinging on their wooden swing which was attached to the arbour pole.

I read somewhere that people who live in places that are more self-sufficient are happier too. Prior to my visit, I'd forgotten what it's like to be surrounded by and soak in the smell of flowers. Just about every balcony has two pots of flowers, which are probably known as 'Guard Flowers,' for each household. A guard flower is important for keeping awareness to the beauty of life.

> **Tip:**
> If you don't have a balcony, put a guard flower on your kitchen window.

When you're mindful, taking a bit of time outdoors every day to surround yourself with greenery and living things can be one of life's greatest pleasures. According to some researchers, gardening is classified as a 'social prescription' which helps improve depression and anxiety levels, even better than prescribed drugs.

Having lots of money is overrated. The law of marginal utility states that satisfaction or benefit from consuming a 'luxurious' product decreases overtime. Even staying in a five-star resort with the best views on a regular basis starts to feel pretty average after some time too. Being exposed to different lifestyles and seeing how people in other parts of the world live is a positive game-changer for many travellers.

> "The Way of Zen.
> Do one thing at a time.
> Do things slowly and mindfully.
> Connect deeply with people and nature.
> Meditate frequently.
> Appreciate silence.
> Expect nothing.
> Be grateful for everything.
> Observe without judgement.
> Consume less, create more.
> Let go of fears and desires.
> Listen to understand, not to respond.
> Be patient and generous.
> Love deeply
> Live simply."
>
> Author Unknown

> "Find pleasure in the ordinary."
>
> Mirjana

Baba Stoya and I went to the local grocers. I never expected to meet a good-looking guy (Maya's and Jenny's cousin) who had finished a nursing degree in a grocery store smaller than a school canteen, but you never know! I felt like history was repeating itself with how my parents met. My dad had finished his nursing course when he met my mum in the shop she worked in. I became even more interested when I heard he also studied philosophy. It told me we were somewhat similar and had similar interests, but it put me off a little when I learnt he was only nineteen years old.

On my way back I met a white fluff ball, a stray dog, along the way. He seemed in his own element and Baba Stoya told me that he was well fed by the neighbourhood.

MIRJANA GLIGOREVIC

> *"Let's get lost in a world made of old books, coffee, camp fires and late-night conversations with people we love."*
>
> Barefootfive.com
> https://www.facebook.com/Barefootfive/photos/a.510982255646701/1480462788698638/

That night, Baba Stoya showed me photos of when my dad was best man at her daughter's wedding. I saw the pride in her when she brought the wedding photos out and she happily reflected on that moment. A picture is worth a thousand words! One photo was slightly discoloured, but it was still just as special to her. That is unlike most people I know, who want to keep up with the latest trends.

Old people keep the memories inside themselves (as opposed to just social media) and that's what keeps the family bonds strong. Thirty years on, she still remembers my dad like her own son. It was so special to see that in today's age, where many families struggle to talk to each other. She'd even had a girlfriend picked for my dad. I could joke blondes aren't really my dad's type, so he had no intention to meet her, but the war across the borders had broken out soon after that wedding.

> *"True inner revolution lives inside your mind and heart, not in the media."*
>
> Mirjana

The photos made me feel like I had dug deep into my family history, and it was so interesting to see what my dad was like before I was born. I also got a sense of what the world was like then. It was a bit of an outdated vibe for me, but so nice to see the old joy and closeness in people. I felt a little sad to see how much my dad had aged compared to then. We are often so busy growing up that we forget our parents are also growing old.

I wonder how many times Baba Stoya looked at those photos over the years?

Day 3

At Baba Stoya's

That morning Baba Stoya approached me in bed with a kiss and said, "Opa Miko." (Woo-hoo Mika!)
She mentioned something that I found amusing. "We from Serbia aren't as kissy and cuddly as you guys from Bosnia." (Mi Srbijanci se ne volimo mazit, ko vi Bosanci).

That told me there are some differences between the Bosnian Serbians and the ones from Serbia. Those little details interest me, but my parents don't like to talk about it due to cultural sensitivity. The people from Serbia find it rather interesting and charming when they recognize it in us.

Auntie Brooke from Montenegro came over for coffee and Baba Stoya took out one of my Australian gifts and showed what she got with such joy. It was a bamboo coaster set featuring Australian animals. It's very easy for people to mix up the echidna with a hedgehog, I would've too before I knew about the echidna. As an advantage, Jenny has a diploma in biology and a very good knowledge about animals. She got out her animal book straight away and explained about the echidna. Having a little bit of background knowledge in the souvenir or item can come to good use.

I learnt even more about some of the Australian animals at Australia Zoo:
- ❖ The platypus is one of only five egg-laying mammals (four species of echidna also lay eggs).
- ❖ The Tasmanian Devil is not known as a 'devil' for having an evil character, but for its teeth and the sound it makes.
- ❖ Kangaroos have two birth canals.
- ❖ The frilled neck lizard could be remains of the dinosaurs.

Most people who value experiences and love to travel would say a plane ticket is the best gift you could give them. On a separate travel trip (to another part of Australia) I was lucky enough to be at Australia Zoo, the home of the original Crocodile Hunter, on Steve Irwin Day, 2019. There was a big shout-out from people who had travelled to Australia Zoo from many other countries that day too.

Steve Irwin was a much-needed gift to Australia, a passionate conservationist who educated the people around him about wild animals.

Why do some people not want to live in Australia?

Some of my friends say because of the big environmental impacts, others say because Australia is full of dangerous animals. Apart from their dangerous looks, did you know the crocodiles keep our waters clean? Surprisingly, watching Steve Irwin's daughter, Bindi, feed the crocodiles didn't look as dangerous in person compared to how Steve portrayed himself on the tv. I had an urge to go up and feed the crocodile too.

Also, according to the late conservationist, the crocodile is a modern-day dinosaur, and Australia is home to the biggest Salt Water Dinosaur. So, it turns out Australia is the country of the dinosaurs!

I feel sure Steve would've gone far to save the environment for many more years to come if he hadn't died so young. He probably wouldn't have wanted to witness all the destruction on our planet though.

I was there when Bindi Irwin repeated her dad's words to the crowd:

> *"I don't care if they remember me, I care if they remember my message."*
> https://www.facebook.com/7NEWSMackay/videos/418107555764201

I asked Auntie Brooke how she felt about Montenegro separating from Serbia. She said, "Of course, it was very sad to all the Serbian people from Montenegro." Auntie Brooke is from a place called Kolašin in central Montenegro, home to all the Serbs.

Indeed, the split was a very sad time, then the referendum came and most non-Serbs voted for independence. It was an example of how a country's citizens who are in the minority are left out sometimes.

> *"Being away from your own country and yet being able to keep traditions and customs is quiet demanding and challenging."*
> Nenad Obradovic (Serbian photographer)
> https://www.facebook.com/Meet.the.Serbs/posts/10158623360494968

It also came up on the news how the other people of Montenegro pushed to eliminate St Sava from their calendar and for the Serbian Orthodox Church to be under the control of the Montenegrin government, not their own patriarchy anymore. That's the first step of a major loss, and where the terrible crisis for the Serbian population of Kosovo started. One separation followed another. Although Serbian was still the official language of Montenegro when I was there, they were in a push to call it Montenegrin. I hope the little bits of the Serbian identity stay well preserved.

My cousins and I were on a mission to learn more about the biggest and most overlooked man in the history of mankind (in my opinion), but I wanted to stop and commemorate the innocent children of the NATO 1999 aggressions first.

MIRJANA GLIGOREVIC

This wouldn't just be my first time visit to the Nikola Tesla Museum, but my cousins' too. Some of my other friends from Belgrade haven't been there either. When something is right at your own doorstep, you often just go past it because you know you can easily go back. I suspect that's one of the reasons many Aussies leave travelling around Australia till last, after they've satisfied their wanderlust for overseas destinations. However, the more you get into the habit of just walking past something, the more you'll also forget to stop and experience it. I was glad all three of us would finally discover the museum.

First, we stopped in Tasmajdan Park, where I went to the headstone to commemorate the victims and left a white (purity) rose with it. The Serbian people really became a target for the world media during the troubles. The media have some brilliant ways of manipulating! My cousin told me about a book, *Jelena* by Milan Kordić. It describes the tragic life of one Serbian girl during the troubles, to whom the media gave an Islamic name to make the world think she was a Bosniak from the opposite side.

That's why I always recommend going with a local tour guide who will give you more of an insight into the whole story, even though a local tour guide will put his own views forward on the story to some extent.

Behind the monument stands the beautiful St Mark's Church, inside which is a replica of the stunning medieval Gračanica Monastery in Kosovo. Rebuilding replicas of some of our historic churches from Kosovo on other parts of Serbian land is a way that some Serbs are trying to come to terms with their great loss of heritage, but nothing is like the original. It brought the common double standards to mind (with the Christian people compared to Muslim), but I'm surprised the United Nations haven't taken it down yet.

I can't even imagine the airstrikes of 1999. People were so frightened by the noises of bombs dropping. Baba Stoya told me how every time she turned on the tv constant warnings for people to get out of the way came on. There was literally nowhere to turn.

In front of the stone monument is a sculpture of three-year-old Milica Rakic. She was sitting on her potty in a bathroom when the bullet plummeted into her head. Since

MY BALKAN HEART

then, she has become the representative face of suffering for seventy-nine other innocent children who died during the bombings. When I touched the statue her angel spirit touched me more than ever. Even my cousins seemed to take a lot of it in as they watched my commemoration. Maya had a tear running down her eye. I think it really got to her at that point, not just for the Serbian children, but for children everywhere.

A war often starts with a conflict between two politicians, who then spread their troubles to the rest of the citizens. It's sad how many other people can fall under the influence of bad politicians though.

Why the bombs? As I understand it, Bill Clinton was angry with Milošević and the Serbian government (who governed the southern state of Kosovo at that time) and their strategy of 'ethnic cleansing' when Milošević planned to place the remaining refugees from the earlier war in Kosovo (their original land). Clinton expressed his anger by bombing Kosovo, in the hope that would bring down Milošević and his plan for cleansing Serbia, adding that it would protect the Albanians.

In an act of aggression called Merciful Angel, the US Army flew daily bombing strikes on Kosovo, 250 over three months. That's more than 500% more than their airstrikes on Iraq and Syria in 2015! Every bit of bad medicine which the Albanians feared before the Kosovo war went onto Serbs with a reverse effect.

I wonder, how can refugees who are left with nothing be a threat to anyone anyway?

Clinton's rival candidate, who lost that USA election, said the Serbian people weren't a threat to anyone and should be left alone.

A lot of people say Milošević was a BIG BAD DOG for causing the war, but I have not come across even one Serbian citizen who doesn't also think of him like that. Yet up to this day, they leave the people of Serbia, from both inside and outside of Serbia, to clean up Milošević's mess. The former President's wife and children have long left Serbia, and know very well they'd be in hot water if they ever tried returning.

After the monument, we got something quick to eat before going into the museum. We sat on a bench under a tree and a bird pooped right in the middle of Jenny's food, a funny moment! We wondered if it was a sign of good luck. I had to

MIRJANA GLIGOREVIC

tell them that I caught a bit of an eye for their cousin from the other day, and they started teasing me, "Oooh, Mirjana has a crush!"

> *"Thousands of geniuses live and die undiscovered..."*
>
> Mark Twain

> *"I'm here to discover one of them..."*
>
> Mirjana

Some scientists him call him 'the God of Science,' others 'the man of lightning,' but I call him The Great Nikola Tesla. European, introverted and a deep thinker, he was everything Thomas Edison wasn't. Despite all his great work, Tesla is an example of how not everyone gets credit for their great work. He powered the modern world with electricity's full potential, but his work is something we take for granted today, unfortunately. Can you imagine our world without modern electricity?

Before we got into the museum, I spontaneously raised how the Croatians think Nikola Tesla is a Croat. The definition of who you are (whether it's based on the country where you live or family origin) also differs in the Western and Eastern countries, as do race and religion.

He came from a traditional Serbian Orthodox family, with an Orthodox priest father, and always identified as a Serb. His childhood home in Croatia was destroyed by the Croatian fascists in WW2 and the stone monuments of eleven of his cousins were destroyed at their gravesite in Croatia, but today the people of Croatia proclaim Tesla as Croatian. I think a lot of small countries try to claim parts from their neighbourhood to make themselves stand out more and get some credit. The controversy around whether Alexander the Great was North Macedonian or Greek Macedonian is another example.

Is the bagpipe Scottish or Irish? Is the pavlova Australian or does it come from the Kiwis?

MY BALKAN HEART

> *"I'm very proud of my Serbian origin and Croatian homeland."*
>
> Nikola Tesla
> https://themindsjournal.com/long-lost-treasure-found-after-116-years-great-nikolateslaslastinterview/?fbclid=IwAR1QuD553DrGZ8mDVR_ghHGFhnjptFX0NYUh5TzZW0injepmkC3Gf8Oqf_A

First, the Nikola Tesla Museum is exceptional for a country that's been struggling to get back on its feet ever since the war. Those who know of Nikola Tesla might just say it's their favourite museum. His work equipment was very old fashioned, but his work is the blueprint of the 21st century Tesla invested his money into making life easier for humanity, unlike Edison—who paid his way to fame when he became the face of the world's biggest electric company.

We accidently turned up to the English time session (more expensive), but I was glad that it taught my cousins that they can understand a lot more English than they think.

The host showed us how Tesla's patents rotate to produce electricity inside the Tesla motor. He was the source of 700 electrical medium functions—light bulbs, turbine engines, electrical rail roads and many more. Did you know the Tesla coil gives us wireless energy?

They turned the coil on, and I took part in a fascinating electrical demonstration. I held a stick that would transmit the volts. So many volts went through the stick and extended down to my body, but I didn't feel a thing! It got me electrocuted in the safest way possible!! Those volts are all around us.

Even today, almost all the electricity in the world is generated by Tesla's system.

He wasn't only a man who was ahead of his time, but a timeless one with his inventions.

MIRJANA GLIGOREVIC

> *"When wireless is perfectly applied the whole earth will be converted into a huge brain, which in fact it is, all things being particles of a real and rhythmic whole. We shall be able to communicate with one another instantly, irrespective of distance. Not only this, but through television and telephony we shall see and hear one another as perfectly as though we were face to face, despite intervening distances of thousands of miles; and the instruments through which we shall be able to do his will be amazingly simple compared with our present telephone. A man will be able to carry one in his vest pocket."*
>
> Nikola Tesla (1926)
> https://www.geekwire.com/2015/nikola-tesla-predicted-smartphones-in-1926-like-a-boss/#:~:text=Yep.,1926%20interview%20with%20Collier's%20magazine.

Nikola Tesla Museum in Belgrade is the only museum in the world where they preserved his original work. He had nowhere to go in the end, either.

Most of today's young generation wouldn't care to look back in time to when/how mysteriously his electricity first came out and compare it to today. Unfortunately, he probably gets less credit for his work from this young generation, whose world revolves around his electric patents far more than our ancestors did.

> *"Whoever leaves a trail of light behind him has accomplished his purpose."*
>
> Mirjana

Tesla's unique way of working was by harnessing the forces of nature, instead of consuming human-made energy. It's such a pity how the wealthy businesses continue ignoring his natural-based solutions, even today when environmental destruction is on the edge of no return. Stephen Hawking (theoretical physicist) was probably right when he said that greed and stupidity are what will end the human race.

In January 1943 the story of Nikola Tesla was ending, but looking out over the Manhattan skyline for one last time, he saw a sky of twinkling lights and a million lives transformed by HIS genius.

> **Three lessons from Nikola Tesla to live by:**
> 1) Money does not represent such a value as men have placed upon it.
> 2) Don't worry if people oppose your ideas (when someone says it can't be done, do it anyway).
> 3) Genius requires solitude.

On our way back we saw a handsome young police officer. I must say he tempted me to ask for a selfie with him, but I didn't know whether it was appropriate. My cousins said it would've been ok. I regretted not doing it at that point!

At the bus ticket station, the ticket-seller asked me, "What's a more liveable country out of Australia or America?" It was hard to answer. I explained everyone has their problems, wherever you go, although some people might be more financially secure. It also felt good to be like a bit of an advisor.

Day 4

Day Tour

We got on the bus for the day tour. As I observed my surroundings, Jenny explained how one side of the street featured graffiti from Grobari (Partizan supporters), and the other side by Delije (Red Star Supporters). I found it interesting how such big rivals (who are like Brazil and Argentina in soccer) were just across the road from each other.

We passed a section where the strong smell of cow manure reminded me, once again, of the different living conditions in a less fortunate country than mine. I was happily surprised though by how many fields of sunflowers I saw along the suburban roads. I read that sunflowers can clean up radioactive waste. They extract pollutants such as radioactive metal contaminants through their roots and store them in their stems and leaves, making them the international symbol of nuclear disarmament.

I don't remember seeing many sunflowers in Australia, but if I could be any plant, it would probably be a sunflower. They not only absorb the brightness of the sun, but also turn to each other and share energy on cold and cloudy days. Perhaps it's something our Australian farmers could consider planting more of in times of drought.

Stay close to everything that feels like good sunshine - feed the positive, starve the negative!

We went to a bar and I had a lemon drink first. I gave a bit of pocket money to the tin 'Serbs for Serbs.' Some people were looking at me oddly, as that's not something they would usually afford. I put 250 Serbian dinars inside the tin, which seemed like a lot, especially with many ten and twenty dinar notes, but it was only equivalent to about $3 AUD.

I saw a guy who was my type. I looked at him for him a few seconds, then remembered how annoyed people in Australia get when I stare at them.

"Sorry for staring, but you're a handsome guy to me!" He was looking at me too, but didn't seem annoyed. He let out a cute Serbian laugh, so attractive!

It might surprise you to see how far you can get in some other countries with $100 AUD. However, I don't think a 1000 local cash note would do much for the locals in another country either. Travel is the only thing you buy that makes you richer, but not even travel has to always be expensive (excluding the flights). Some of my workmates from Australia say they travel the outer world because inbound travel in Australia adds up to a lot more with the accommodation costs and some experiences.

Maya said to me, very apologetically, that she couldn't afford to take me to a restaurant. She could buy me a drink, but restaurant food was a luxury experience for them. "No worries at all," I said. What I had planned I knew was an unmissable experience, so if my cousins couldn't afford to take me, I was more than happy to pay for them.

It was a five-star dining experience. As we were taking in the beautiful panorama of the city from the rooftop restaurant, Maya said, "I never thought I would come to something like this in a million years!" It surely was an experience above and beyond, with a perfect city view. I also couldn't have felt more rewarded to provide my cousins with something they usually wouldn't be able to afford. You will live a perfect day when you do something for someone who will never be able to afford to repay you.

> *"To be happy is to share happiness with those around you."*
>
> Mirjana

What made it even better was that we had the space all to ourselves. There were two other tourists sitting at the other side of the hotel, and the woman came to take a photo of the three of us. They had travelled all the way from New Zealand. I didn't expect people from a non-local background to come to Belgrade from New Zealand. It is a pristine country with so much natural beauty and a variety of everything, but did you notice how New Zealand often gets left out from the world map? (Probably because it's very separated from the rest of the world.)

I wasn't very impressed with the Karadjordje steak I had for dinner, but the picture-perfect view from the hotel amazed us. (I figured from some personal experience and feedback from other travellers that best food and best view don't often go together. It's usually one or the other.)

My cousins wanted the photo on Instagram, but taking my other relatives of a lower living income into consideration, I was cautious about publicising a 'luxury experience' not everyone could afford. Maya then told me how they're the lowest of all, and she cleans every weekend for a living. So, she's qualified in high-level law, but cleans for a living?

A job is a job, whether you're a doctor or a cleaner. None of us have the right to mock another just because you're earning more money than them. We are all trying to put food on our table.

> *"Some of the most generous people have no money. Some of the wisest people have no education. Some of the kindest people were hurt the most."*
>
> Steve Wentworth
> https://twitter.com/tinybuddha/status/1141394008729690112?lang=en

It was my first major eye-opener of how low-caring the government is, and how it leaves people out. Mind you, it touched me. In Australia it's getting harder and harder to find a job. Everyone wants someone with many years of experience, but you need a chance to build up the experience too. And no one knows what the job market will be like after the Covid-19 lockdown.

I was also reminded that social media photos don't always resemble reality, as everyone makes their lives look much better on social media.

MY BALKAN HEART

Life is not perfect, but it has perfect moments. You're likely to encounter them on your travels. That moment you take in a perfect view from a peak point, explore an exotic place, or meet people who open your eyes—that's just one thing I like about travel.

> *"Social media is training us to compare our lives, instead of appreciating everything we have. No wonder why everyone is so depressed."*
>
> Bill Murray
> https://www.reddit.com/r/QuotesPorn/comments/8r8dn2/social_media_is_training_us_to_compare_our_lives/

When I unexpectedly heard the church bells strike at 8pm in the middle of our talk, it felt even more magical. Maya took me to the other side of the hotel later to show me one of the biggest football stadium matches. She said, "Film it and show it to Dad. He would be so proud." My dad was named in honour of a late Red Star Player. I found out that most of my cousins go for Partizan, but my dad goes for Red Star. I didn't see the actual match, but saw the light reflecting up and heard the players singing their anthem—they were as loud as fireworks! It wasn't the best tasting food that night, but will probably be one of my most memorable dining experiences.

When we left the hotel my cousins kept walking, wanting to spend more time in the city. Walking in the city that late is something I'm not used to in Melbourne, where I live, so I was sceptical at first. I don't think locals of Belgrade look at the time or mind the dark. There were still lots of people around, and they didn't even look sleepy. It probably made Belgrade feel safer than Melbourne at night, but it woke up a big sense of freedom in me more than anything. The feeling of awakening inside you is probably one of the most powerful gifts you'll get, wherever you travel.

You know you've made the right decision when there is peace in your heart and freedom in your soul. I felt like a free spirit who could just roam anywhere and do anything, anytime, in this big wide world.

MIRJANA GLIGOREVIC

"Go where joy invites you,
Where it ignites you,
And reminds you
what it means to be alive."

Harpeet M Dayal

@stardustpoetry

"To move, to breathe, to fly, to float,
To gain all while you give,
To roam the roads of lands remote,
To travel is to live."

Hans Christian Anderson

https://backroadplanet.com/project/travel-live/

For the Travelling Foodies:

Belgrade is very meat-based, so vegetarians probably won't get the most authentic food experience, but I still invite you to Belgrade.

Directory for the best vegan restaurants in Belgrade:
https://theculturetrip.com/europe/serbia/articles/the-6-best-vegan-restaurants-in-belgrade-serbia/

We do have a good vegan rice called Đuveč (pronounced Joo-vach) with sautéd veggies and our traditional Ajvar seasoning. We also have a unique potato salad with Spanish onion and oil/vinegar dressing.

Tip:
Global Vegan by Ellie Bullen is a good vegan guide book for travellers.

MY BALKAN HEART

> **Top Dishes to Try in Serbia:**
>
> **Pljeskavica:**
> Traditonal chicken shnitzel with melted cheese and more flavour
> **Karadjordje Steak:**
> Rolled veal or pork, stuffed with sour cream, then breaded and deep-fried.
> **Cevapi:**
> Handmade sausages from minced meat, with a bit of cheese and onion.
> **Sarma:**
> Traditional cabbage rolls with minced meat, rice and other seasonings.
> **Burek:**
> A flaky, meat-filled pastry with yogurt, also one of the most popular foods in the Balkans. You'll find it in most bakeries.

Another unique thing about Belgrade: If there's anything open late at night other than restaurants and the usual tourist stuff, it is bookshops. On the way home I got distracted by one and had to go in. My cousins found a great book for me called *The Little Prince* and got it as a gift for me. It was originally French, but over time has been translated into 150 languages.

The book talks about the meaning of life from a child's point of view, but reminds adults to count the stars instead of money. It might take me back to my childlike mind, or at least remind me of what life was like when I was a child.

> *"Returning to innocence, childlike sense of wonder and joy, I am allowing myself to trust the process of life again."*
>
> Asia Boros
> https://www.instagram.com/p/CAdS5kinqQh/

You have many parts of yourself, creative, analytical, spiritual, wise, etc., but this book emphasises the childlike. Unleashing your inner child might just be the key to healing into wholeness, unity consciousness and complete integration of the ego.

To return to a childlike sense of wonder, fun and innocence would be awesome. I want to be one of those people with a childlike spirit, even after much time has passed and my physical body is older.

Think about it:

> *"It's funny how so much of 'finding yourself' in adulthood is simply getting back to who you were and what you loved as a child."*
>
> Mirjana

It made me think—what a great book to read when I get back into the hustle and bustle of adult life and worrying about paying off the mortgage. Also, a good book to refresh me on Cyrillics (traditional Serbian dialect). I only knew Cyrillic before I came to Australia, but since then have learnt the Latin dialect quickly and forgot the Cyrillic.

Serbian children learn to read and write two different dialects from a young school age, so I could make a joke, "they're the smartest kids in the world."

The store offered a bookshop catalogue for 1 Serbian Dinar. I honestly thought I would find nothing for 1 Dinar when 1 AUD=73.27 Dinars. Most people only used it to sit on when they were waiting for the bus back home, but no one cared about 1 Dinar.

On our way home on the city bus, a neighbour tapped Maya on the back and asked if they had heard what happened in Bosnia. Their parents (Uncle Nick and Aunt Maree) had been in a car accident, along with Uncle Mick and Auntie Lila. She said the collision happened at a roundabout in Bosnia. It was such a shock, a big reminder not to take anything for granted. You never know when the last goodbye will come.

How many people have you heard of that have or are fighting cancer, but remain in very good spirits?

Sadly, it often takes something big to happen for people to start counting their blessings, using time wisely and living life to the fullest.

Should we see tomorrow as one day more or one day less?

We got into panic mode before making a phone call and double-checking everything was ok. Luckily, it was nothing major. Aunt Maree had slightly hit her elbow and had a bruise, while Auntie Lila hit her head a bit.

> *"Don't wait for something to happen to start living life to the fullest."*
>
> Mirjana

Day 4

Prime Hotel

Jenny and I went to the hotel where my guided tour would start from. We arrived early and met up with my lovely friend Daria, a Slovakian girl I met online through my autism support group. Serbs usually kiss each other on the cheeks as a symbol of respect at the start, but Daria was hesitant on touch. However, I still found her very charming.

She is an above-average mathematician who cleverly diagnosed herself with Autism Spectrum Disorder. It felt so good to meet another girl on the spectrum, and in a place where most people seem to lack awareness about it more than in Australia. She brought me a paper-made flower inside her slum hat, reminding me of how people in the olden days used to bow down to royalty. The purple flower was a very nice match with my purple bag, but she chose that colour for another reason. Like many people on the spectrum, Daria also has Synesthesia (a condition where people connect more than one sense to a particular picture or object), and a shade of purple is what she envisioned with my name. *That just goes to show how strong our senses and sensory issues can be.*

I thought that my friend resembled an old granny (with her hat and glasses), so I had an urge to tell her that she looks like one. I said sorry in case she didn't like my comment. A Neuro Typical (a person who doesn't have autism) is much more likely get offended by it, but as a girl on the spectrum too, Daria knew what I meant and said for me, "*Retro.*"

Many autists can understand each other's neurodiverse language naturally. That is one of the reasons people on the spectrum don't like to be in big crowds of people who are off the spectrum.

Like me, she also likes to travel and value experiences, so I got her a travel journal where she could write her memories. Daria described the time she was floating high in the sky in a hot air balloon in Germany and spotted lots of little kids waving up to her from down below as one of her favourite travel experiences. That's rather like something out of a storybook for me. Little kids are part of the beauty in this world too. She (Daria) is one of the few people happy with how life is in Serbia, and she feels she has a sense of purpose with helping people there.

Maya soon dropped by too after work, and we talked a bit about cultural differences. She asked Daria if it's a tradition to play happy songs at Slovakian funerals, as she had attended the funeral of a Slovakian woman who was killed by her man. It also reminded me of how the traditions in different countries vary and have different meanings. For example, while Serbian funerals are all about mourning of the person who died, Australian ones are about the celebration of the person's life.

I also asked Daria how her family did in the 90's war, if they'd had it easier because they were a different race. I had heard that some places were safer than others. My mum is from one of the harder hit places, a small Orthodox village on the borderline of Bosnia and Croatia. An easy target for the Croatians, and I felt a lot of empathy for Mum's side of the family from that moment. The Catholic army took the Orthodox people away in WW2, and then again in 1992. It's so sad. Her destroyed childhood village was more of a ghost town with a graveyard when I strolled through it in 2010. Mum is a born survivor. I probably got that from her, and that is probably part of how I overcame so much in the past.

We went for a quick lunch across the street, then went back to my hotel room. A hot day, I was so tired from the humidity I just dropped my luggage down and threw myself on the bed straight away. After the three of them went home and I was left in the room 'on my own,' the nerve-wracking feeling of 'all alone now' kicked in for me.

I'd rather it happens in my home city than elsewhere though. Solo arrivals to other countries will probably feel less daunting from now on, because I know what it's like to be a solo traveler. People on the spectrum function much better when they're well informed before an event.

> **Tip:**
> You can stay in a hostel if that make the experience less scary.
>
> If you get an extra day, visit the Museum of Illusions for fun.

The rest of my tour group arrived in Serbia by plane within a few hours, but I didn't meet them until the next morning.

Morning Treat

At Belgrade Square with Maya.
(National Museum of Serbia behind us.)

Sightseeing Belgrade from Belgrade Square.

MIRJANA GLIGOREVIC

At President Tito's gravesite.

Maya and I with the statue of Tito.

With the cousins in Tasmjanski Park.

MY BALKAN HEART

Paying tribute to the innocent children of 1999.

At Nikola Tesla Museum.

Receiving voltage from the Tesla Coil.

With cousin Jenny at Nikola Tesla Museum.

MIRJANA GLIGOREVIC

First visit to the St Sava Temple.

On Hotel Crystal Rooftop.

By Parliment Building at night.

MY BALKAN HEART

The Tour – Day 1

Tour Sets Off

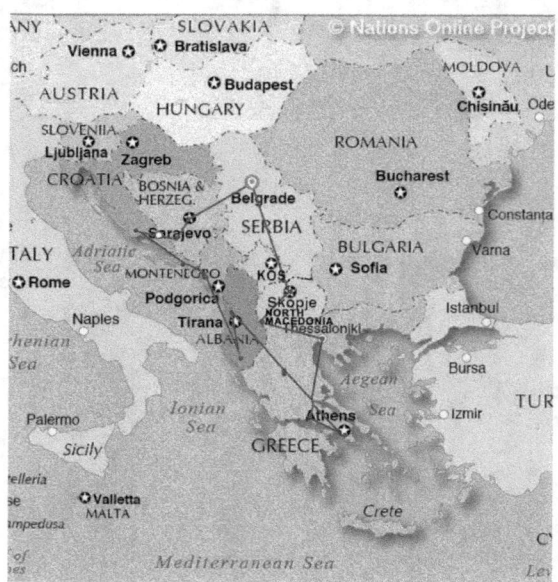

The tour consisted of me, two British women (mother and daughter), and an Egyptian gentleman from Canada. We had a driver who looked very much like Željko Joksimović, the famous singer who represented Serbia twice on Eurovision. I was thinking I could've almost taken a selfie with him and put on Facebook that I came across him.

Our tour guide, Dejan, looked Aussie to me with his reddish hair and beard.

I went into Tito's museum and House of Flowers for the second time, but now with a tour group. Yes, he was a much-loved president in most of Yugoslavia (especially with Bosnian people), but the one thing the tour guide didn't mention was the war between Chetniks (King's side) and Partisans (a communist side). There is always more of a story behind everything, but tour guides will always put their views forward.

I was wondering how Tito came to be buried there, when Serbian people are more divided about him than any other Former Yugoslav country. I learnt that Tito asked to be buried in Tito's House of Flowers, as it was his favourite place where he often went to relax. Today, there are even petitions trending amongst the Serbian people to remove Tito's gravesite from Belgrade, as many think he played a big part in Kosovo's separation from Serbia. It goes to show how political views and values also change.

St Sava Temple is the second biggest Orthodox temple in the world. When I was there parts of it were still under construction, but more recently a big, beautiful image of St Sava, made from 15 000 mosaic pieces, was added, completing the temple. That means travellers can now witness it in its full beauty. Some travellers say it reminds them of the Hagia Sophia in Istanbul.

Walking into St Sava Temple for the second time, I stumbled and fell on cracked tiles. Once again, it was a sad reminder of not only the damage and effects of war, but how selfish the government is, for they have failed to invest in fixing it up ever since.

> *"Never let a stumble in the road be the end of the journey."*
>
> Unknown

People often get confused between a church and a temple in that context. A temple is a place for worshipping a God figure or saint, while the church is a place where they hold the assembly. However, the temple of St Sava also holds church services.

When you get inside, the first part is a monastery, a very peaceful place for reflection and obediences. St Sava was a Serbian Prince who was also an Orthodox monk, the first archbishop of the autocephalous Serbian Orthodox Church, a writer, the founder of Serbian law, and a diplomat. It's almost hard to believe how one man could have been so many things! He will always be a Patron Saint of Serbia.

The Serbian Orthodox church achieved autocephalous status in 1219 and the leader of Constantinople (the former capital of the Eastern Orthodox empire) had assigned St Sava to be the first Archbishop of Serbia. After St Sava's death in 1346, Emperor Dušan elevated St Sava's church to the rank of the Patriarchate. His place was the Patriarchate of Pec in Southern Serbia (today's Kosovo).

The middle part of the temple is so divine and consists of real gold inside. It is where the liturgy takes place on Christmas and Easter and couples can also marry. The big, beautiful chandelier on the ceiling represents crown.

In times of early Christianity, the Catholic people spread the message of faith with crosses and the Orthodox people with icons or frescoes. That's why a lot of Orthodox churches are bigger. If you like frescoes and art, an Orthodox church is the place to visit. A local guide took us through the stories of the saints on those frescoes and some other temple items.

The Belgrade Fortress, Kalemegdan Park

> *Belgrade is the city at the confluence of the Sava and Danube Rivers, where a lot of different civilisations sailed to over time - the Romans, Obri, Huns, Hungarians, Turks, Austrians and Germans, just to name a few. They all contributed to building the structure throughout different eras.*

Such a strategic position destined the fate of the city which was fought for in over 115 different war battles and was destroyed 44 times.

They fought relentlessly, and whoever ruled at the time used the fortress and resources for their own military stronghold and advantage. The gates and fortresses are a symbol of constant battle, strength and persistence for the Serbian people who haven't left Belgrade over time. Kalemegdan comes from the ancient Turkish words kale, meaning fortress, and megdan, meaning battlefield.

Historically, I learnt warriors had some brilliant strategies for dangerous times. The tour guide showed us holes at the top from shooting, but the shooters couldn't get through the wall because it was constructed from a very strong steel structure.

They even had their own little underground world (underground museum today) where they would train and prepare. For example, they connected the ridges of steel in such a way they could burn them when the attackers tried to intrude. I would describe it as 'The Secrets of the Underground.' Inside some gates were military vehicles and armour weapons.

The Romans originally built the Belgrade Fortress, but others destroyed it and rebuilt it, repeatedly, for sixteen centuries! The Turks conquered it in 1521 and held onto it for the next 300 years, before surrendering in 1867. From then, the city of Belgrade became predominantly Christian again. The Belgrade Fortress still stands today above the confluence of the Danube and Sava Rivers, and for many is a symbol of Serbia's capital and endurance.

We went through the King's Gate to the Upper Town. Taking in the beautiful scenery at the banks of the Danube and Sava Rivers, I sensed the oldness of the city. The Danube River is the second biggest river in the world and flows through ten European countries. It connects Belgrade with the North Sea on one side and the Black sea on the other, thus the different invaders came from both directions. They probably sailed like the Vikings did thousands of years ago, but I saw the river with such serenity. Looking to both sides felt incredibly peaceful.

> *"A woman in harmony with her spirit is like a river flowing. She goes where she will, without pretence, and arrives at her destination prepared to be herself and only herself."*
>
> Maya Angelou
> https://feministquotes.tumblr.com/post/25044228834/a-woman-in-harmony-with-her-spirit-is-like-a-river

MY BALKAN HEART

Water doesn't simply become a river though. It has to take many different forms before joining with the river. Just like the raindrop, the stream and the river, you too are meant to become many different people on your way to yourself.

> *"For the raindrop, joy is in entering the river-/Unbearable pain becomes its own cure."*
>
> 18th century Urdu Poet, Ghalib

The Victor Statue has been standing above the banks of the two rivers since 1928, and represents Serbia's victory over the Ottoman and Austro-Hungarian Empires during the Balkan Wars and WW1. The sword facing down in one hand represents 'end of fighting,' and the bird of peace in his other hand faces those countries and represents a time of peace and reconciliation.

That history is something many countries forget to take into consideration about the Serbs since the breakup of Yugoslavia. While the Serbian population was higher in statistics and the people spread out through a good amount of land in the former Yugoslav country in the last civil war, outsiders have erased the fact that they were allies in both world wars and saved many innocent lives. That is also why they were the last to acknowledge the breakup of Yugoslavia.

Daria brought to my attention one particular historic event that highlighted the humanitarian side of many Serbs. In 1885, Serbia became the first country in history to put the war with another country on hold by letting the Bulgarian aid transport pass safely through their own territory. It motivated the International Red Cross authority in Geneva, Switzerland, to put up a sign with the motto 'Be as humane as a Serb in 1885'.

I stopped to take a photo in front of the Sahat clock and tower. Sahat (Clock) Gate was built in the 17th century by Andrea Cornar, during the repair of the then damaged southeastern walls. She originally worked under Austrian authorities, but continued when the Turks hijacked Belgrade.

After so many battles, Part 3 of Kalemegdan was made into a beautiful walking park (see the map).

I was soaking in all the greenery and serenity as I walked between the grass and the big tree.

I kind of started the tour back to front, but if you started exploring Kalemegdan Park from Knez Mihailova Street, you would never guess such battles had taken place while in the midst of the green park.

We ended the tour on the other side of the park, just in front of Knez Mihailova Street. The tour guide pointed out the library, under which the Romans dug out the white ridges which they built the Belgrade Fortress on, and named the city after 'Beo-grad' (White city). However, Belgrade isn't the only White City in the world. We also know Arequipa in Peru as the White City. Just goes to show how big this world is and gives us less of a reason to stay in one place!

From the park, the driver gave us a bit of time to explore Knez Mihailova Street on our own. Other than the significant history, the street is also most famous for eating, shopping, etc.

> **Travel Tip:**
>
> Walk from Knez Mihailova street to Zeleni Venac (Green market) and catch a bus to Branko's Bridge. Cross the bridge for the best overall view of Kalemegdan.
>
> If you like architecture, take a walk to Terazije Square and discover some beautifully designed hotels, including Hotel Moskva (Moscow) and Hotel Balkan. Around the corner from the Green Market is Amsterdam Hotel too.
>
> **For wheelchair users:** Use an electric wheelchair to get over cobble stone surfaces.

I looked for somewhere I could have lunch in Knez Mihailova and asked a few locals for advice.

One man said to me, "*I recognise that your accent is from the south.*" (Probably because of my ijekavica accent).

"Not exactly from the south, but from Republic of Srpska," I replied.

"I'll show you where they make good cevapi, and the restaurant owner is also from Bosnia," he offered.

As I was on my way back, a guy who helped fundraise for people with Cerebral Palsy approached me. He explained the cause, and I smiled and said, *"You chose me because you saw the way I walk, didn't you?"*

"You have it only with one leg, a lot of the people I work with are in a wheelchair," he replied.

I gave, it would've probably been embarrassing if I didn't, so he took me to the exchange office to exchange my Euros. There's always someone worse off than you. I gave a little bit back to the children of Banjica, a hospital I often used to go to from Bosnia for check-ups. That hospital from my childhood is how I remember and built a connection with Belgrade.

I couldn't find my mates or my driver, so I figured out that I was lost. The driver had gone without me! There was probably a misunderstanding between us, or I took too long to have lunch. I nervously walked from Knez Mihailova street through the whole Kalemegdan complex.

My group mates and the driver were nowhere in sight. One of my biggest fears was getting lost on my solo trip and this was probably one of my biggest moments of feeling lost.

I didn't know what to do, so I went back and forth between the Knez Mihailova street and Kalemegdan.

Walking all on my own again, I looked up to the sky and spotted some birds. If you're lucky enough, you might even spot a squirrel in the park, but I didn't on that occasion.

> *"Did you know Serbia covers less than 1% of Europe, but is home to 51% of fish, 67% of mammals, and 74% of birds in Europe?"*
>
> #Interestingdailyfacts

I think most travel lovers are birds by spirit animals. Birds roam freely with their wings and use landmarks and big building structures to navigate their way.

MIRJANA GLIGOREVIC

One of my friends said to me:

> *"Your nest is at home, but really, I know that you want to and can spread your wings.*
> *If you watch a bird's nature, you will see they conquer wind, rain, storms, etc., and still continue flying free.*
> *You have that inner strength to conquer, no matter what's thrown at you. You're stronger than you think."*
>
> — Elise Wright

As I continued on my wild goose chase and looking out for them at every angle, I came to what I thought was the end of the park. That was the last corner, but around it, I spotted something fascinating—the Zindan Gate! The structure has a real medieval feel to it and is one of the most popular photo spots. I probably wouldn't have seen it otherwise, and wanted to have a photo with it, but my group was still nowhere to be seen. At that point, I was too nervous to take any more steps forward in case I got even more lost. That was my *'what did I get myself into?'* moment. If I'm so lost in my home city already, how on earth will I manage in the many unknown places to come?

My photo of the gate alone still felt like some accomplishment though, and a good memory to look back on.

> *"Sometimes you find yourself in the middle of nowhere, and sometimes in the middle of nowhere you find yourself."*
>
> — Mirjana

One friend told me of a great book called *Exposure*, a travel tale about a man with certain psychological challenges. He feared too much and struggled to get out of bed, until he reconsidered a new travel lifestyle that shed a light on him. I could also relate to the song *Superman (It's not Easy)!*

The Belgrade Zoo was just across the road from where I had been standing for a good amount of time. There I found out my city is home to some of the rarest beauties in the world, including a white lion couple and a white tiger couple.

Not knowing what to do, I just went back to Knez Mihailova Street, inside the shopping centre where there were lots of people. I let my cousin know what had happened, and she told me to catch a taxi.

I didn't have the sim card to call the taxi, so I searched by foot. The first one was very expensive and I couldn't take it. I asked if there were any more nearby—yes, two streets away. The anxiety of being out of place once again kicked in. By the time I had walked to the second taxi by foot I was so sore and exhausted, but glad I'd found it.

When I got to the ATM once again, I felt the stress from being inexperienced. I was too scared to put my card in the machine in case it didn't work. I took all the dinars I had out of my wallet and counted them instead.

I think the taxi driver saw I was stressed and inexperienced, so was happy to give me a slight discount. It was all good, and I got back to the hotel safely.

It gave me a great sense of accomplishment, as I'm usually not a good problem solver.

MIRJANA GLIGOREVIC

Me and my friend Daria

Inside St Sava Temple.

Kalemegdan Complex

The Tour – Day 2

Niš, Skopje

It would've been nice to stop at Vrnjačka Banja along the way (Serbia's most famous spa, between Belgrade and Niš), but we drove a long way, straight to Niš. I stayed with the driver so I wouldn't get lost again, while my teammates went more into the centre.

I didn't get to the centre of the city, but expect I would have seen Serbia's third biggest city as more of a third world country style. It was surprising to witness the old infrastructure and such hard living conditions in this part of Serbia. I was fascinated when I spotted a man travelling on a horse-drawn wagon, it told me they still take on things from their ancestors.

Niš is a city where significant battles against the Ottomans took place. However, The Niš Fortress stands today, with a statue of Milan Obrenović, who contributed to freeing the Serbian Christians from the Ottomans. Vojvoda Sinđelić was another outstanding revolutionary commander who sacrificed his own life, as did his army, for the future generations. The Ottomans put all the skulls of his soldiers in Ćele Kula (the Skull Tower) where they remain today. It is a very daunting place to go to today and an experience that will shake a Serb to their core. If anyone ever goes there, I would definitely advise them to go and relax in the therapeutic waters in the spa of Niš straight after, or at least soak your feet. Those thermal spring waters are not only soothing for the skin, but the heart too.

On the positive side (across the road from Ćele Kula), is a mountain where the natural features come together over summer and form the facial figure of Vojvoda Sinđelić. Many Serbs believe nature did its job and saved the Duke from oblivion.

My Muslim group member from Canada found the Niš Fortress interesting, as did I. Equally fascinating was that although Muslims and Christians fought in that period many years ago, we were now open to freely discuss all about the Ottoman empire with no conflict.

Did you know Niš was the birthplace of Emperor Constantine?

> *"I love places that make you realize how tiny you and your problems are."*
>
> Anonymous
> https://themindsjournal.com/i-love-places-that-make-you-realize-how-tiny-you-and-your-problems-are/

I took the opportunity to ask George, the driver, one-on-one, "How's the economy and the living state of people in Macedonia?"

He replied, "It's not good with the Albanians taking over a lot."

It was one of those things you wouldn't say to just anyone, other than to your own people. It also reminded me of the Serbian people in Kosovo. I did say it's sad how whoever is the original always ends up losing their own land. However, my next tour guide would be an Albanian from Macedonia, and I wasn't going to let that get in the way of me enjoying my trip. At that point I felt Mother Teresa's quote applied very well in her own country.

> *"If you judge people, you have no time to love them."*
>
> https://medium.com/@cioviewssocial/if-you-judge-people-you-have-no-time-to-love-them-24be48a40c9

Skopje Hotel: Best Western Hotel Turist

> My next place was the Land of the Rising Sun (North Macedonia). It was late afternoon by the time we got to the capital, Skopje.

I was lethargic from the long road trip, but wanted to make the most of my time. Feeling uncomfortable exploring alone in a brand-new place, I asked the two lovely British ladies (a mother and daughter) if I could join them when they went out. They rang my hotel room prior to the outing.

The girl asked me, "Do you know what that says?" and I translated for them. I felt somewhat of a help identifying the place we were looking for, and that's where my knowledge of Cyrillic came in handy.

We went to the Museum of Macedonian Struggle. It told the story of how the Macedonian people fought for their independence through different eras, and the leaders who achieved it. It was interesting, but a shame when the tour guide talked too fast and made it difficult to understand!

I liked the layout of the story and the artistic details in the sculptures though.

I honestly thought Serbians and Macedonians had better political relationships, as they're neighbours with the same religion, so it took me by surprise when I learnt that the leaders who fought for Macedonia's independence had opposed us frequently. Outside the museum I took a photo with the statue of the Bulgarian boatmen who played an important role in helping Macedonia rise against the Ottomans.

Skopje probably has one of the most unusual road structures. I knew the fancy lane between the Vardar bridge and the restaurants section was for walkers and cyclists, but no one would guess cars! As I was returning from the bridge side, a car came out of nowhere, one of the most frightening experiences! Such moments make a good travel story, I guess. I watched in amazement at how all the road users use a small lane—all together! Don't unexpect your 'unexpected' in another country!

MIRJANA GLIGOREVIC

It was probably the name more than anything, but I couldn't resist having a Mother Teresa meal for dinner. The British mother said one thing that surprised her from Serbia to Macedonia was how many cornfields there were. My *Book of General Knowledge* says corn is the most eaten food around the world, followed by rice. I focused on my food until the daughter got up to capture the pink evening sunset on her camera. It was like Neverland (from *Peter Pan*) when I looked up at the sky. The going down of the sun was a very enchanting moment, and it will probably be even more beautiful when the sun rises again tomorrow.

> *"The sun is a daily reminder that we too can rise again from the darkness, that we too can shine our own light."*
>
> S. Ajna
>
> https://www.goodreads.com/quotes/8726727-the-sun-is-a-daily-reminder-that-we-too-can

> *"Reset with every sunset and refresh with every sunrise."*
>
> Mirjana

The Tour - Day 3

Guided Tour in Skopje, Day 1

Skopje is the city of statues. With a statue at just about every corner, it felt like there were more statues than people in that small-populated country.

I was hoping to hear more about Alexander the Great, one of the most important rulers in history who conquered the Macedonian Empire. I knew the Macedonian Empire was huge, stretching all the way from Greece to Persia, and comprised many small sections with different names, but the one thing I learned is that Alexander the Great was Ancient Macedonian (Greek), not Slavic Macedonian (from my understanding at least). Nevertheless, Skopje still has reminders and statues of Alexander the Great everywhere.

One of the most famous statues of Alexander the Great on the uprising horse in Skopje emphasises all his glory, although he eventually lost.

Europe's oldest bridge connects the Macedonia Square on the right bank and The Old Skopje Bazaar on the left bank. The number of mosques in the bazaar took me by surprise.

Did you know the Nazis tried to abolish the Vardar Bridge in WW2, until some clever locals prevented them?

The new part of Skopje formed much later, but the old and new bits are all so jumbled up it's hard to separate them. I found myself in the world capital of kitsch (crazy).

Macedonia and Greece still have some disputes over the name, but they have come a step forward in agreeing to name the former Yugoslav Republic of Macedonia 'North Macedonia.'

MIRJANA GLIGOREVIC

We went to the home of Mother Teresa, one of the most loved people of all time. If there's one thing I like about the Albanian people, it's probably her. She also had a kind and caring heart like me, and often stopped to help the less fortunate. Her mother taught her the importance of charity from a young age, and at twelve years old she devoted her life to religion. Her life changed when she got a call to help the poorest of the poor in India, and later she became the Saint of Calcutta.

People threw rocks at Mother Teresa for her religion, but her reputation grew as she opened hospitals for those dying of HIV/Aids, tuberculosis and leprosy, and orphanages, and she won the Nobel Peace prize in 1979. Then again, I also came across articles that said she did some not nice things but went around just to spread her religion. There's some controversy to many things in life, I guess. I find it interesting though how she and Princess Diana, who were both well known for their humanitarian work, died in the same year.

MY BALKAN HEART

Where I was almost hit by the car.

Statue of Alexander the Great.

Skopje Vardar Bridge.

Mother Teresa's Home.

Inside Mother Teresa's home.

Tallest Christian Cross.

Kale Fortress

The Tour - Day 4

Guided Tour in Skopje, Day 2

While I always knew Macedonia to be a predominantly Christian country, the centre of Skopje consists of many mosques and most things are Islamic based. Everything is mixed up in Skopje, the old with the new, and there's no rule of what goes where. I could totally understand why Skopje is known as the world's 'capital of kitsch.'

We had a good walk through the Skopje Bazaar, where I spotted my first beautiful postcard and decided I would start collecting them from each place from then on. Postcards give us an opportunity to re-live the place, and I use the back to write my favourite memory from each one. Every place is special in its own way. I have made like a little recipe book with my postcards and I can just flip from one page (place) to another.

I also learnt something Serbians and Macedonians have in common - opanke - traditional leather shoes with curled up toes.

After the bazaar, I took the hard walk to the Vardar Hill to explore the Kale Fortress (also known as the Skopje Fortress), which sits on the highest point in the city and overlooks the Vardar River. The fortress location is incorporated into the North Macedonian flag. It was a very long and exhausting walk up, but worth reaching the majestic, medieval fortress. When I came to the top of the hill and the sight of the fortress suddenly appeared, it felt like it emerged out of nowhere. The Kale Fortress was home to some of the most powerful emperors, in a very discreet place amongst the mountains.

MIRJANA GLIGOREVIC

The mountains provided a place of refuge and hiding from the Ottoman for many Christian communities, and that is one of the two theories of the meaning of the word Balkans.

Balkans: a region of mountains.

Originally built by the Orthodox Emperor, then destroyed during several wars against the East Roman Empire, the Kale Fortress was further constructed during the 10th and 11th centuries from the remains of other Orthodox fortresses by adding additional walls to protect the lost Roman city. In 1346, Stefan Dušan was crowned Emperor of Serbs and Greeks inside the Kale Fortress. It was where he kept Dušan's Code - the plan to legislate different areas of the kingdom and to make a stronger bond between the Serbian state and the newly conquered cities and regions. It was used in the Middle Ages and by the churches during the Turkish occupation. The code also had punishment procedures for those who didn't respect the rules of the church.

> *"A queen knows how to build her empire with the same stones that were thrown at her. She will always turn pain into power."*
>
> Author Unknown

From the other side, on top of the Vodno Mountain, stands the tallest Millennium Cross in the world for 2000 years of Christianity. Across the road from the fortress was an Ottoman village. Travis (English tour guide) mentioned that, "The Ottomans didn't destroy churches, but turned them into mosques." However, Christian families in those times knew turning it into a mosque was part of destroying the church, as the church no longer served its purpose. It felt like they had lost a part of their origin and themselves, just like with many Serbs in Kosovo today. (Travis was the general English tour guide who travelled with us to each destination from Macedonia. We also had a local tour guide for each place. Travis often introduced us to a place before we got out of the van, and at times added more information to the local guide's talks. We had two guides for most of the overall tour.)

Dušan the Mighty also constructed the Dečani Monastery (gift of his father). His most important was the Holy Archangels Monastery near Prizren, Kosovo, where they buried him.

Kosovo is the foundation on which we have built our values that made us into the people we are today, and the place of our original sacrifices. That is why many Serbs refer to Kosovo as 'the heart of Serbia' and will probably never stop hurting over their great loss.

The last time I checked, a lot of the countries that refused to accept Kosovo's independence are the ones who know what it's like to lose your place of origin and true identity. They're Cyprus (North Cyprus), Russia (Chechnya), Spain (Basques) China (Taiwan), India (Kashmir) and so on. Kosovo's Independence will also make it harder for many other countries that are currently fighting against irredentism. When the new Islamic structure became a tourist attraction many years later, it was a more popular and beautiful attraction than the old for many tourists. However, very few tourists acknowledge the true history behind it. For example, an online travel friend of mine who's been to Cyprus said she found the churches that had been turned into mosques much more interesting than just the churches themselves.

Kosovo has also become a popular tourist attraction since it gained independence. Many people have expressed a desire to go there, but visiting the south part of Serbia was not in any non-locals' interest prior to that. The 6% of remaining Serbs in Kosovo today are in the fight against oblivion.

Since 1999:
- More than 200,000 Serbs have been expelled from Kosovo.
- More than 150 churches and monasteries have been destroyed, damaged or desecrated, of which 61 were monuments of culture.
- More than 10,000 icons, ecclesiastical art and liturgical objects have been stolen and sold on the black market and through auction houses around the world.
- 5,261 tombstones in 256 Serbian Orthodox cemeteries have been damaged or destroyed.

The Serbs who are left in Kosovo today are not only in the fight against oblivion, but are trapped in the most inhumane circumstances. More recently, the Albanian border police have completely banned all other Serbs from entering Kosovo directly too.

The poem Crven cvete (Red Peony) was written by Jelena Bojović in a refugee convoy from Kosovo and Metohija, and tells a story about the suffering of the Serbian people in that region from the great Battle of Kosovo to the present day. The red flower is the Kosovo peony, which according to legend sprang from the blood of Serbian heroes, so symbolizes the Serbian suffering and blood spilled throughout history, and the hope that never dies.

My peony,
Buried beneath deep grass,
There's no way to reach out to you.
The bird Kosovo is hiding my tear with its wing.
No one had permission to take you away from me,
But I'm begging you...
For the heroes of our pride,
For the glory of the Serbian nation,
For every girl's happiness,
And God's blessing.
Don't let me leave you,
Without your cross and glory,
Don't let St. Vitus Day's name or my name
Disappear from here.
My flower...
The midnight trembles all of the heroes, who pray to God
To bring back down our shining star,
Re-birth with the faith of Christ,
Gračanica, Devič, Dečani and Zočište villages.
Can I return...
To the Paštrik mountain,
Home of the lambs
I will feed them,
The messengers to my darling.
He still carries the sword of truth
In the name of love.
Restoring our church on a cloud
Where we will marry
My flower...
Hey,
The angels will bring my church back down.
In the middle of the old white town of Dušan's city,
I'll find Metohija, my shining star,
Stay safe in God's hands.
Oh, my Peony (flower),
I would sacrifice my life for you,
If I could use this hand to pick you.

You can hear the original song at: https://vimeo.com/141731881

MIRJANA GLIGOREVIC

My *Book of General Knowledge* stated that the people of Aleppo have inhabited the region for 8000 years—no other city has been inhabited for longer. A UNCHR report has also stated that the war in Syria has lasted longer than WW2. Remember there are two sides to every story. I imagine the Indigenous population of the US and Australia would be against Kosovo parting from Serbia too, for they would understand the loss.

> "Serbia is a temple and Kosovo and Metohija is an altar. Without an altar, the temple loses its purpose and its sense of existence. Serbia is a body and Kosovo is the heart in that body. If the heart is torn from the body, it remains a decaying corpse."
>
> Bishop of Artemia
> https://www.helsinki.org.rs/doc/HB-No148.pdf

The Western world (English-speaking countries) will always be prone to being influenced by American media and powers, while the East will stay on Russia's side. That's why there is a big division on political issues in this world, and the Western side has heard very little about the huge sufferings from war in Syria from the side that had Russia behind them.

The statue of Miloš Obilić (a Serbian knight from the 14th Century) is one of the very few that survived an assassination attempt of all Christian remains in Kosovo from Albanian irredentists. Kosovo wasn't on our itinerary, but Travis wanted to take us to Kosovo too. I knew he would take us through many recently constructed mosques that have replaced the churches. I said nothing, for the obvious reasons, but deep down I was happy I didn't have to go there and dive into the pain of every Serb.

For more information look up a documentary:
Kosovo: A Moment In Civilization
https://vimeo.com/ondemand/kosovo

MY BALKAN HEART

Prince Mihailo's hand on his statue in Belgrade has pointed to Prizren (the imperial city of medieval Serbia, province of Kosovo and Metohija) since 1882, when there were no Albanians in Kosovo.

According to an online documentary I watched, prior to the 90's war the Albanian population in Kosovo was 66%, and Serbian families have between one and three kids on average, while Albanian families usually comprise four to ten kids. Then came the NATO aggressions on the Serbian population.

While talking to someone who has a less emotional outlook on it, I gathered that the takeover of Albanian language and culture could've been less or more expected with such a big rise in Albanian population to 94%. However, if there ever comes a time when the Serbs become the asylum seekers from any other countries, it would be nice of the Albanians to let them back in to Kosovo, just like the Serbs let the Albanians in throughout history.

In 2017 there was a big move of asylum seekers from the Middle East to Europe. Many European countries have put up electric fences to keep asylum seekers out. In March 2016 the borders of Slovenia, Macedonia and Croatia closed, marking the official end of the Balkan route, causing thousands of refugees from the Middle East to become stuck in Greece and Serbia. The Australian news described it as the world's worst humanitarian crisis, but Serbia was one of the few countries who let the asylum seekers in and provided them with shelter. Today, some locals in Serbia fear overpopulation with those ethnicities too.

Sometimes it's hard to draw the line between minding your own business, free speech, facts and racism. If I were to express a concern with overpopulation of some race in Australia, I would probably come across as racist. It's the same for the 6% of Serbian population in Kosovo today who got trapped under Albanian control and live a very hard life as second-class citizens on Serbian land.

Kosovo is the blackbird's land (Kos), but also known as a battlefield. That is where we became strong warriors even after being knocked down in many wars, and another reason most Serbians refer to Kosovo as 'the heart of Serbia,' although over 90% of our remains have vanished. I'm surprised at how the few Serbian landmarks, the statue of

Miloš Obilić in Gračanica and the Medieval Tower in Kosovo Polje, survived the assassination attempts of all Serbian remains in Kosovo.

If you had the opportunity to visit the Serbian monastery of Gračanica in Kosovo and Metohija, and stand in front of that witness of Serbia's glorious past, would you wish you could hug it just as you would a person dear to you? The members of Ensemble Venac did just that a couple of years ago, when they danced Serbian kolo (folk dance) and showed all the beauty of Serbian tradition.

That night I had a late dinner at my Skopje hotel. The chef I talked to was very nice, with a cheerful spirit. I spoke in my language and he spoke to me in his, but it was pretty much the same and I felt like he was one of my own people too. His Greek Salad was very yum, and when I put cash out in front of him, he merrily denied with the words, "No cost tonight." It must've been my lucky night.

The Tour - Day 5

Ohrid

Hotel: Belvedere Hotel

Today was my first time I visited a mosque in Tetovo (Macedonia). Tetovo is a city in Macedonia that's home to lots of Albanians.

As we were driving to Ohrid, I saw an Albanian flag and got confused.
"Are we in Macedonia or Albania?" I asked Travis.
"Still in Macedonia," he said.
"How come there was an Albanian flag?" I asked.
"Because the law states if you have over 50% of another ethnicity living in a place, they can put up the flag of their ethnic country," he said. I guess that goes to show the challenges that come with overpopulation with a certain ethnicity, not just in Macedonia but worldwide. Also, the pressure to remain silent about some things.
By the time I got to Ohrid I was very sunburnt and had to put a scarf over my neck. I started talking to one of the hotel workers in English. When he saw my passport ID, he said, "Jel ne znas pricati Srpski?" (Do you not know how to speak Serbian?)
I smiled and said in Serbian/Macedonian, "I do know, but I also know that Serbian and Macedonian aren't exactly the same."
The Bulgarians conquered the city in 867, and Ohrid became the capital stronghold of the Bulgarian and Orthodox Empire in 990. Bulgarian Patriarchate later fell under the

authority of the Ecumenical Patriarch of Constantinople. If you like churches, Ohrid is the place for you!

Ohrid originally had 365 churches, one for each day of the year, and each Orthodox church had their own archbishop. By the 16th century the Bulgarian Empire reached its peak and rose above many other Orthodox districts. Our first major stops were in front of the Church of Saints Clement and Panteleimon. Saint Clement was Bulgarian and the most prominent disciple of St Cyril and Methodius, who spread the Orthodox faith with the Cyrillic scripture throughout Eastern Europe. They built the church in 893, where St Clement educated over 3,500 Orthodox disciples.

Next, we went inside the beautiful Orthodox Church of St Sofia. The walls were as blue as the sky and the saints on those walls showed how religion, art and colour can mix and match to produce great beauty. Some frescoes had faded a bit, but the beautiful feeling of originality came to me. It made me understand the Serbian pain and connection to the destroyed churches in Kosovo even more.

I was sad they allowed no photos inside, but didn't want to break the rules. That's where the beauty of the Internet comes in. I will find the photos of the inside and pass them on from an online resource. To respect a place and culture is to put their local rules ahead of your desires.

I also lit a candle to honour the deceased Christians during the time of the Ottomans, although it melted quickly. As we were leaving the church, I spotted something very unexpected. A baby turtlewas crawling slowly on church grass and enjoying the sun. It's eas y to forget that taking baby steps is also a way to move forward. Direction is more important than speed. Don't discourage anyone who keeps going forward—slow and steady wins the race!

> **How to be a Responsible Traveller:**
>
> Check the website https://smartraveller.gov.au and follow the destination related advice and safety regulations.
>
> Respect local rules.
>
> If something makes you question whether something is ethical or unethical, trust your gut instinct and say no.
>
> Leave a positive ecological footprint.
>
> **Extra tip:**
> Carry a biodegradable straw. Drinking out of a pasta straw sounds like a cool experience in Italy.

Next, we went for a ride on Lake Ohrid, one of the most beautiful lakes I've ever seen. For a moment, I thought it was the place I want to retire in! Gentle lakes like this are a good alternative to beaches for people with a physical condition or balance problems. You can still soak in the beautiful scenery and enjoy the peaceful water vibes and activities, but the waves don't come crashing at you. Lake Como in Italy is another example.

    I thought my parents were exaggerating about the beauty close to their own homeland because they have seen little of the world, but you have to see it to believe it. Then again, I sensed it would be nice, but not exactly the same, if I hadn't come from the other side of the world with a tour guide and saw the place on a bigger scale with a few other places too. A picture is worth a thousand words, but sometimes the picture can't describe the beauty of the landmark in reality either. I wish I could reflect exactly on what made me fall in love with Lake Ohrid when I look at the photo, but to come back to the place is the only way. If you want a full, beautiful view of Lake Ohrid, climb and look from Tsar Samuel's Fortress. The Church of St. John at Kaneo, along the lake, is the most picturesque and outstanding church of all.

MIRJANA GLIGOREVIC

We got on one of their original boats, known as čamac. It reminded me of my childhood, when we went to the River Bosna and saw people floating on it, and how happiness comes in small packages once again. If I were on a big cruise ship, I wouldn't have been on the water to catch the beautiful views from the best angles. Floating and relaxing on the green water was just as beautiful, and I tried hard to get a nice landscape photo of the church and lake together.

Halfway through my cruise, I spotted something that looked so magical—a man lying on his boat in the middle of the lake. He couldn't have looked more relaxed, comfortably sunbathing while snoozing underneath his hat. There was beauty in every corner he could turn to. The only way I could describe what I saw is Lost in Paradise. If there's any heaven on earth, this would probably be it.

When I was getting off the boat, the driver, who spoke Macedonian and could not speak English with the other tourists, asked me about my background. After the boat ride we (the tour group) sat for dinner together and I had a moussaka. Eat, Pray, Love in Ohrid.

dance
as though no one is watching you,

love
as though you've never been hurt before,

sing
as though no one can hear you,

live
as though heaven is on earth

souza

"Jobs fill your pocket. Adventures fill your soul."

Jaime Lyn Beatty

https://www.goodreads.com/quotes/3231638-jobs-fill-your-pocket-adventures-fill-your-soul

We also had a little time to explore the Ohrid Bazaar and town centre. I walked across the riviera to discover beautiful necklaces and bracelets made from their local pearls. It was their specialty, made of those scarce stones and gems. I was thinking how much my mum would like looking through all the shop windows, and it tempted me to get her something she'd adore. She's more of a gems and pearls than a diamonds type of girl.

Bird's-eye view of Ohrid.

Entry into Church Town.

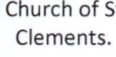

Church of St Clements.

MIRJANA GLIGOREVIC

St Sofia Church interior.

Inside St Neum's Church.

Sailing on Lake Ohrid.

MY BALKAN HEART

Bird's-eye view of Lake Ohrid.

Pituresque Lake Ohrid.

Lake Village

MIRJANA GLIGOREVIC

The Tour - Day 6

Ohrid - Thessaloniki (sleep in Thessaloniki)

Hotel: Tobacco Hotel

Some music well-known to me came up on the radio and I was the only one who could understand it. It was music to my ears!

Although the official languages of Bosnia, Serbia and Croatia have different names, they're still the same language with just a few different words. Music is one of the few things that continues to unify the three different constituent groups. It doesn't matter what nationality the singer is when the listener can understand the words, feel the connection and enjoy the melody. The positive and healing effects of music apply to everyone.

Some of the most heartfelt music for me comes from a beautiful, young Macedonian singer called Toše Proeski. He was 'rich and famous,' but a very humble soul who often made songs about needing very little in this big world. His time on earth was very short, but the music he left behind continues to touch me deeply every time I listen to it.

As we were going through the mountain regions, I sensed the peace of the people who lived there. Each house keeps within a certain distance of one another, but just enough not to feel isolated, and I sensed that mountain people received far less pressure by the standards of the society. It felt like a very peaceful place for me to live in.

> *"Destroy negative energy with the power of music!"*
>
> Author Unknown
> https://www.pinterest.com.au/pin/794463190486986449/

I had a bit of trouble getting out of Macedonia, as the border control hadn't stamped my passport on the way in. Luckily, they found me in the system. However, the moment I got to Greece, it felt like a second home. The hotel guy pronounced my name perfectly, including the 'j' that English-speaking natives get wrong. My hotel room was colourful and I saw angels when I looked up at the ceiling.

> *"Measure life by the number of stamps in your passport."*
>
> Mirjana

MIRJANA GLIGOREVIC

The Tour - Day 7

Thessaloniki - Delphi (Athens sleep)

Hotel: Athenaeum Grand Hotel

We visited one of the most famous ancient museums in the world, Delphi Archaeological Museum. But I was also sad, knowing it would be my last day with a great, small group of people.

Prior to the Roman Empire, Ancient Greece was the most important civilisation in the world.

First, the guide explained the lifestyle of people who used to live underground in those times. Ancient Greek society valued individual freedom, sport, learning and the arts. Apollo was the god of art, music and poetry, and many other Emperor's praised Apollo by giving him a statue of themselves. There are many statues, including the famous Charioteer of Delphi.

When you're a history fanatic like me, you're too busy taking notes of what the guide is saying, but some statues (including the Kleobis and Biton and the Sphinx of Naxos) reminded me of Egypt. It made me realise the connection and influence pharaohs of Egypt probably had on the wider world during the time of Ancient Greece. Travellers will find statues of pharaohs and Roman emperors in other countries that were also influenced by the Greek and Roman Empires. I was surprised to find an Egyptian one in Croatia too.

The Delphi museum holds many sculptures of pharaohs, emperors, and carved sculptures which tell the story of the Ancient Greek civilisation, but the most famous one on display is the Golden Piece of Apollo. Ancient Greece and Rome were very colourful, so amongst many bronze sculptures is a little white lie too. Classical Renaissance statues were originally also very colourful, but the colour faded with time. Other Renaissance artists started imitating the first statues, in 'white' too, and many generations followed. When the time of Ancient Greece was coming to an end, Emperor Nero transferred 700 statues from Greece to Rome to try to unite to unite the two civilisations through the same veneration.

After the museum, we went outside to Mount Parnassus to see the actual Temple of Apollo. The sacred symbol of Delphi, the omphalos (navel) that signified the centre of the earth was kept in Apollo's temple, and one copy remains inside the museum today.

I had a few stumbles and one fall along the way, but was still very intrigued by many historic monuments I passed, including a stadium of Delphi which the Roman's constructed.

The Delphi experience also brought back to me my first ever flight, on Olympia airline, when I was immigrating to Australia in 2002. Athens was my first stop over.

Did you know the original Olympic games were held in honour of Zeus?

MIRJANA GLIGOREVIC

MY BALKAN HEART

Ancient Greek World.

Golden piece of Apollo.

MIRJANA GLIGOREVIC

On my way to Mount Parnassus.

View along the way.

Another mountain view.

The Tour - Day 8

Athens Attractions

Attractions I saw:
- ❖ Parthenon
- ❖ Temple of Athena Nike
- ❖ Acropolis Museum
- ❖ Temple of Goddess Athena
- ❖ Famous stadium.

> **TIP:**
> Getting up at dawn is the key to getting authentic travel photos with just you in place.
> If you're an early bird, use the chance to march behind the soldiers and watch their morning ritual of rising of the Greek flag up behind the Parthenon. Get up every morning and remind yourself: I CAN do this!

Today is not just a new day, it's a new opportunity, a new chance and a new beginning. Embrace it. I started the sunny morning by embracing the perfect view of the Parthenon from my hotel.

The amount of work and attention to detail that went into that type of building is unbelievable. Looking at the 3000-year-old temple brought out the spiritual energy within me, and a sense of what it would've been like thousands of years ago. Something like this is what you need in the morning to motivate, inspire, and give you a sense of peace.

MIRJANA GLIGOREVIC

Horrible bushfires had affected Greece just a few weeks prior to my visit, but I knew the Greek people were also like mine, so I wanted to give something back to them. I gave some random victims postcards with a beautiful message of hope.

The song below was originally made-up by a Bosniak singer for the Balkan flood victims, but I think it goes for many other hardships in life too.

A rose blossoms in every garden It always finds a way through!	Ένα τριαντάφυλλο μεγαλώνει σε κάθε κήπο Και υπάρχει πάντα
We keep you in our thoughts and prayers from Australia.	κάτι που θα το βοηθήσει να ανθίσει
From Mirjana, your sister in Australia xxx	Σας κρατάμε στις σκέψεις και τις προσευχές μας από την Αυστραλία. xxx

Nikola Tesla spoke about how energy is all around us. Life craves energy, but subconsciously we will always choose the path with the least resistance. That's why high calorie food tastes better and why we feel more depressed when there is no sunshine.

When you have Cerebral Palsy, it also takes a lot longer for the muscles to warm-up or to get the blood flowing prior to a work-out. I have to push myself to go to the gym sometimes, but having a bigger purpose in front of it really helps. For me, that's destination travel!

My personal trainer told me everyone has some level of fitness, even if they don't know it.

Mindset is important when working-out. Don't just look at exercises as a punishment for a poor lifestyle/body, but a celebration of what you can do. Reward is stepping-up to the next level.

> **Did you know?**
> Eating two bananas in the morning can help you sustain enough energy for a 90-minute work-out.

Sports psychologists say goal-setting techniques are important to improving your performance. If you know of a personal trainer who's an experienced traveller too, they can be a good source of advice for the physical demands of your specific destination and set you up with a good exercise routine to prepare for it. My PT knew there were lots of stairs in Greece and gave me some stepping exercises. Bananas are good energy boosters for a long day of walking, and two can sustain your body for a 90-minute workout.

> **Fitness Tip:**
> Pair up with a friend if that makes your training sessions more enjoyable.

> *"While outcome goals refer to the intended result, process goals shift the focus instead onto the things you need to do in order to achieve the outcome. The idea is that if you focus on the process, the outcome will follow."*
> Dr Melissa Weinberg, School of Psychology, Deakin University
> https://this.deakin.edu.au/self-improvement/how-goal-setting-can-put-you-on-the-path-to-success

Science has also confirmed that you absorb energy from the people you hang around with, so stay away from toxic people.

MIRJANA GLIGOREVIC

> *"Five Types of People to be Around:*
> *The Inspired.*
> *The Motivated.*
> *The Open-Minded.*
> *The Passionate.*
> *The Grateful."*
>
> Author Unknown

When you're on a mission to discover the significant history, there's no better place to start than in a 3,400-year-old city such as Athens, but it was a big shame the tour guide spoke too fast and I could hardly understand her!

> **Interesting Fact:**
> Democracy, which gave the right to vote on law to citizens, was actually established in Athens around 500 BC.

I met up with my new group mates, two brothers from Malaysia who started their tour in Greece. We drove in a mini bus from that point. While driving through the streets of Athens, I saw graffiti still there from the 2015 economic protests. It was pretty much everywhere. Some reviews describe Athens as a 'big, dirty city,' but I didn't let that stop me from having a good time. I think one way to know your heart is made to travel is when you embrace all the elements that make up a place as part of its unique beauty and authentic experience, instead of approaching it with a negative attitude (e.g., even when the taxi driver always comes late). According to a lot of frequent travellers I spoke to, the more unique a place is the more you'll love it. Some common favourites have been India and Morocco.

As we quickly passed the Arch of Hadrian along the way, I was lucky enough to capture it on camera. We went to the Acropolis (the big rock), where they had built all the sculptures from limestone. The ground surfaces were very rocky and uneven, so it was another big physical challenge for me. My first stop to take a photo was in front of the world's most famous stadium—Panathenaic Stadium.

We went past a few more rocks and I stopped in front of the Old Temple of Athena, where the people used to pray to the Goddess of Wisdom. Classical Greek architecture is amazing. The purpose of those columns was to support the standing structures, but they are so beautifully decorated and detailed from the top that you can almost guess they're just pieces of art. Greek use of the golden ratio has surely produced a unique and beautiful outcome. One of their most outstanding architectural pieces is the Porch of Maidens (featuring six female figures) on the north side of the Erechtheum. They were a picture of elegance with the pottery on top of their heads.

I wasn't sure how she got there, but it felt amazing to see an old woman in a wheelchair on the sturdy Acropolis ground too. Later I read that the Acropolis has a wheelchair accessible entrance, which may be reached via an elevator/lift. You can get to the elevator after taking a wheelchair stair climber, which has a platform to load your chair securely.

I also came across an article where the researchers state that Ancient Greeks used to purposely build ramps at some temples for people with a disability who needed religious healing.

https://www.livescience.com/ancient-greek-temples-disability-ramps.html?utm_source=Selligent&utm_medium=email&utm_campaign=9160&utm_content=LVS_newsletter%20&utm_term=3611752&m_i=Mf2hZPYUtfvkD2Sw7IRjQS59LNu%2BxjEiCg4stiQwe16RGSStiAPoBb8HGDRe9rYP8__knUxXi1gqME48641jVwI85zoU4tr4wBRsnJMMM3&fbclid=IwAR0bSCb4OOiqcE4cTqX78Scp0Qolg6gIbtO4EQKe8qS7IJGvGj5T1D_bcpA

Even though some attractions may be physically demanding, more and more are starting to accommodate people with a disability, whether it's by a lift or a ramp entry. Starting and stopping halfway, or going up to get a nice view, is better than dismissing the whole experience, but going the whole way is always better if you can.

Next was the Parthenon. I thought Uluru in Australia was the only sacred rock in the world, but the Parthenon is the sacred rock of Greece. While the rest of the group went to the other side to see The Temple of Athena Nike, I stayed and rested in my current section. The other part of the Acropolis was too rocky and hazardous for me. One thing that surprised me about the Acropolis was the many big limestone rocks everywhere. Why they were everywhere? Were they part of the design or what? Apparently, they are construction parts that didn't succeed according to plan or make it throughout the century, however the archaeologists didn't want to take them away.

Every master was once a beginner, but according to some researchers it takes a beginner 10,000 hours of experience before he officially becomes a master. It was one of the bumpiest roads I've ever been on. I might've had a few stumbles—but I didn't fall once! Getting past each of those stones was a success!

> *"The best way to treat obstacles is to use them as stepping-stones. Laugh at them, tread on them, and let them lead you to something better."*
>
> Enid Blyton
> https://www.goodreads.com/quotes/630657-the-best-way-to-treat-obstacles-is-to-use-them

Night

Under the Acropolis is the Plaka, also known as the neighbourhood of Greek Gods. It can be hard to find, but the tour guide told us we stayed in a good spot near the Plaka, so I wasted no time searching for it later in the day.

I kept asking locals for help with, "Do you speak English?" while searching for it by foot. Every few metres I stopped and asked a local to give me directions. Don't feel embarrassed to ask for help, for no one expects you to know everything as a tourist. Learning the basic words, including manners, can go a long way with cultural respect to the locals of your destination though.

> *"I can't change the direction of the wind, but I can adjust my sails to always reach my destination."*
>
> Jimmy Dean
> https://www.brainyquote.com/quotes/jimmy_dean_131287

I'll share a funny story from my home city, Melbourne. I asked a woman who was a European tourist about some location, and she laughed from embarrassment of not knowing the answer. She didn't know I was the local one though.

It was when I found the main Plaka district and sat for dinner that I felt my first major accomplishment as a solo traveller outside my homeland.

People on the spectrum are used to feeling completely out of place, but at least in a foreign country it's expected! I felt the most lost in Serbia, and almost got hit by a car in Macedonia, but as I drifted further away from home, I also felt oddly more in place, or more comfortable in a way, too.

I started getting comfortable with being uncomfortable in the middle of my tour.

> *"Comfort can become badly addictive, but not when you reach it like this. Travel is probably the healthiest addiction."*
>
> Mirjana

Travel Tip:
Remember to use Google Maps if you need a step-by-step guide from point A to B.

Plaka district was like a little village within a city. I love those places that are like two in one, such as a remote place, but with many elements of a city.

I love the narrow little streets where there's a lot to explore, but were designed for pedestrians, like the Knez Mihailova in Belgrade. These places with great architecture, lovely pedestrian streets, delicious food and a vibrant atmosphere could be good for romance too. I had Greek-style sandwiches for dinner, followed by one of the best pancakes in Europe, probably. Although pancakes are very international, each country makes them in its own unique way. Japanese ones are probably the fluffiest. Banana crepes are a Thai version of a pancake. My mum bought me the best ones from a Khao Lak market, but only in Bangkok will you find the $1.50 ones.

Although streets don't always look the most appealing, they often have the best foods. If you can't afford to travel, I would definitely recommend the nearest food market. Taste the unique ingredients of different countries until you come to the best taste. All the different pancakes I tried were yum! Even coffee has different criteria in different places. Italian Mochaccino is the next one on my 'to try' list.

As I was waiting for my food, I gave my second card to a person who had suffered in the Greek bushfires a few months prior.

I met a thirty-four-year-old guy who was interested in me. He was beyond my years, but seemed very flamboyant and young at heart. It was the first time I ever felt admired by a guy. It was a lovely feeling, but it also made me feel lost. He asked me for my social media details and I kind of froze in place. He even offered to take me out one-on-one after the restaurant.

Many travellers say that people usually feel more comfortable approaching you and starting a conversation if you're solo. French men have a unique way of appealing to everyone though, including married women, by bringing them flowers or chocolate. A former travel agent told me she saw a lot of handsome men in Buenos Aires, but there's no rule where you would find them. I also read a very sad story about how a man took his wife to Paris for a divorce.

Heartbreak is one of the hardest things to go through, but travel can help mend a broken heart. I read a magazine article about Katy Collins, the girl who used her heartbreak to help her write great travel novels. Since her fiancé said no to walking down the aisle with her, she's published her travel stories on three different destinations. You can find them at The Lonely Hearts Travel Club. I also read an article about a senior couple who went backpacking to forty countries and fell in love all over again.

Staying solo, I went down further to explore the Plaka suburb deeper.

I passed so many shops with Orthodox icons and could understand why it was known as the Neighbourhood of Greek Gods.

There are fifteen Eastern Orthodox churches, but I found that some people in Australia refer to the Orthodox Easter as "Greek Orthodox," which can make some non-Greek Orthodox people feel left out. Other examples are Serbian Orthodox, Macedonian Orthodox, Russian Orthodox, Romanian Orthodox, Bulgarian Orthodox and more, although many of those church leaders wanted an independent church government over time, unfortunately.

The more I walked through Plaka, the more I realised just how similar all Orthodox icons and vigil lamps are. I could say that I was in a 'Neighbourhood of My Gods' too.

Most Orthodox people do look up to the same Saints though, and most family homes have an icon of their own Patron Saint on the wall with the vigil lamp as a sign of blessing.

I stopped and went into one shop that had a bit of everything, where I spotted a nice floral scarf my mum would love, and got it for her. The lady there told me the same thing in Greek three times, but I couldn't understand her. I was wondering why I was standing quite a while without proceeding, until I learnt a new cultural standard. They have a system of processing items where the first person takes the price ticket off and puts it in a little bag before they pass it on to the second person, who you pay. Athens Guide website says the shopping experience in those streets is like shopping on one of the Greek islands, so I guess I had a bit of a taste of the Greek islands on the mainland of Greece too.

Places of worship, eateries and shops are the main places where different cultural etiquettes apply. It's a good idea to observe how the locals do it first.

MY BALKAN HEART

View of the Acropolis from my hotel.

Hadrian's Arch

Poster on a Greek building.

Herodes Atticus Theatre.

MIRJANA GLIGOREVIC

The Erechtheion where King Erechtheus lived.

The other side of the Erechtheion.

The Parthenon

Plaka district

Humble Orthodox home beauty.

The Tour - Day 9

Athens - Meteora

Hotel: Antoniadis Hotel (Kalambaka)

> **Coddiwomple:**
> To travel purposefully toward an as-yet-unknown destination.

While the Greek islands such as Santorini and Mykonos may be the best known for tourism, don't under-estimate lesser-known jewels on the mainland of Greece too.

I went with a travel company called Fez Travel, who specialised in Greece and took me through the less-known beauties. To my advantage, the maximum number of people in my group was six, and there was also a general English guide who could assist me, along with a local tour guide in each place. My need to keep up with others was far less than in some bigger groups, and the general English guide was very helpful.

> To find out how Intrepid Company can help travellers with a disability, visit:
> https://www.intrepidtravel.com/au/accessible-tours-travel

During the long drive to Meteora, we passed a lot of beautiful beaches on the mainland of Greece. I also used the big road trip to meet my new Malaysian mates and talk about how things are in their country. I learnt a bit about the history, including how a lot of Chinese and Indian people immigrated to Malaysia to work in the threading industry.

MIRJANA GLIGOREVIC

Meteora is a place I didn't know much about prior to my visit; I treated it like just another add-on to my tour. But that day I was on a mission to discover one of the most enchanting monasteries in the world. It's one of the few places where natural beauty blends in with monasteries and religious tradition (apart from Ostrog in Montenegro). However, in Meteora the pinnacles feel much more surreal.

First, how a lot of stall holders picked up on the Serbian language and used it with many other tourists fascinated me. To be somewhere different, outside of your own country, but with such significance to your origin, is special. To come from the other side of the world to discover it—that's amazing.

> *"Be sure to make room for unknown adventure."*
>
> Mirjana

It wasn't the first time I'd heard from other travellers that the places which you least expect take your breath away the most. The Emperor of Serbs and Greeks, Jovan Uros, was one of the main builders of the Holy Monastery of the Great Meteora after he became a monk and moved to Meteora in the 14th century. That explains why a lot of Serbian tourists go there.

The view of the big rock from down the bottom was more like a mediaeval castle. It sure felt like I was climbing up to a castle rather than a monastery as I climbed up so many stairs!

Going up 140 steps was very painful for me, but I refused to give up. I couldn't start, then stop halfway, to something so beautiful. Don't let the entire staircase overwhelm you. Just focus on that first step. (One step at a time.)

> *"Remember to look up at the stars and not down at your feet."*
>
> Stephen Hawking
> https://www.goodreads.com/quotes/490245-remember-to-look-up-at-the-stars-and-not-down

Strength doesn't come from what you can do. Strength grows in the moments when you think you can't go on, but you keep going anyway. When the tour guide noticed I had a 'disability' she offered me a walking stick, but I didn't want to go below my usual walking standard.

Overcoming a big physical challenge makes you perfect in your imperfections, happy in your pain and strong in your weakness. Get comfortable being uncomfortable. Get confident being uncertain. Don't give up just because something is hard. Pushing through challenges makes you grow.

> *"It is not the mountain we conquer, but ourselves."*
>
> Edmund Hillary
> https://www.brainyquote.com/quotes/edmund_hillary_104652

I really had to get to the top to witness it and believe it. It was like fantasy came to life, a place out of this world!

What can I say? Keep your head and your heart going in the right direction and you will not have to worry about your feet. I can't describe the feeling of success and accomplishment.

The pinnacles at the top are just perfect, a realistic setting for science fiction or a fairy tale. The top of those huge pinnacles was a discreet setting for the Orthodox monasteries and a safe-haven to the Eastern Orthodox community against the Ottomans. Originally, twenty-four monasteries were built, but only six remain today.

We explored The Holy Monastery of the Great Meteora, also known as The Transfiguration of Our Saviour. Inside, the walls are all covered with frescoes that tell the story of early Christian suffering. It felt like those frescoes came to life in a way. I've been to both (Catholic and Orthodox church) and I'm not being bias just because I'm Orthodox myself, but I think that it feels more divine inside an Orthodox church and the frescoes touch you on a deeper level than the crosses in a Catholic Church. (I think a lot of elderly get more drawn to God as they approach their last stages of life on earth, anyway.)

The tour guide took us through the differences between the Catholic and the Orthodox church structures. The front part of the Orthodox church is the reception/entrance, the middle section is the prayer space, and the altar is the paradise which only the pope has access to. In the Orthodox church the pope usually performs the mass from behind the altar. He is usually married before he becomes a pope, which brings the natural family connections closer compared to those outside the family. Confession for things like murder is also more questionable.

All in all, I still think the Catholic and Orthodox beliefs and values are mostly the same.

Greeks are the only Orthodox people who celebrate Christmas according to the Gregorian calendar with all other Christian people, but celebrate Easter according to the Julian calendar, on the same day as Orthodox people. There are a lot of different interpretations going around with religion, but I get annoyed when people don't understand how the different denominations of Christianity relate to each other. I went to a Catholic school and remember mentioning how we're Christians and got the reply from the rest of the class, "We're not Christian, we're Catholic." And then there are those who say Christian and Catholic is the same thing.

Christianity consists of a number of denominations. Catholic is one denomination, Orthodox is another. The bottom line is that if you believe in Christ as the son of God, you're a Christian, no matter what denomination you are.

The major difference between the Orthodox and Catholic people took place when the big Roman Empire split into two. The West Roman Empire comprised Catholics, and the East Roman Orthodox people. St Peter and St Paul were the main Apostles for both denominations. They had frescoes of both in the Holy Monastery of the Great Meteora. The visit to Meteora opened up my desire to visit St Peter's Basilica in Rome too. Visiting a country of a different faith can bring you closer to your own faith. I always used to associate monks and temples with Buddhism, but the more you travel the world the more you see how different religions relate to each other.

After exiting the temple, I found myself on the edge of the huge cliff at the other end. I looked down at the epic bird's eye view of the landscape below, a testimony of how high I'd come.

> *"The Edge: There is no honest way to explain it because the only people who really know where it is are the ones who have gone over."*
>
> Hunter. S Thompson
> https://www.goodreads.com/quotes/604368-the-edge-there-is-no-honest-way-to-explain-it-because

The guide told us about the monks who still live in the temple across the other side. They get up early in the morning and have prayer time at about 4 pm. We also talked about the Christian burial principles with the Greek tour guide, and with Travis about how they differ to Islam.

By the time I had taken a good photo it was a shame we couldn't enter the section where the monks pray. Their prayer time had come. I felt bad that I held my photographer friend up, especially when I heard so many people around us yell, "Please, this is a once in a lifetime experience." It's a good idea to use those chances.

I heard Travis talking about the good quality of mountain water, so I filled up my drink bottle from a tap high in the mountains. It's not just the water quality, but the air and a mountain lifestyle are great for your wellbeing. Some people can feel their lungs opening up with the change of air. That's why Switzerland is high on my travel list, and I look forward to seeing what I can take from life over there.

It took me by surprise when I looked at the world map of countries who do and don't have access to safe tap water, or even water. More than half of the world doesn't consume water safely. It was peculiar when I had to adapt to just bottled water on my overseas trip to Thailand, but I still wouldn't exchange my other wonderful travel experiences which I could only get in Thailand, including elephant bathing, bamboo rafting, and the turtle sanctuary. Relying on bottled water in Thailand also set the tone for my future travels in other less fortunate countries, which also have beauty worth exploring.

> *"Once a year, go someplace you've never been before."*
>
> Dalai Lama XIV
> https://www.goodreads.com/quotes/7354400-once-a-year-go-some-place-you-ve-never-been-before

I took a few more minutes to soak in the surrounding views from the top of the mountain, and to take more photos.

No wonder it was almost impossible to build. Even from the top, it felt more like a castle until I got inside the monastery.

> **Omnism:**
> The belief that no religion is truth, but that the truth is found within them all.

Even if you don't have a connection with some place or religion, some feelings might just come up at a certain place and time. One of my friends, who's now a protagonist, told me how she felt a change inside her when her auntie took her with the cousins to an Orthodox church where they lit the candles for the deceased and she got an icon for a gift. Although there's probably only one heaven and one earth, different countries have different versions of their pathway to heaven according to their own religion. Each of these places brings out some spiritual sensation though, and I felt the same when I visited The Big Buddha temple in Thailand.

The Stairway to Heaven hike in Hawaii (Haiku Stairs) is one of the most popular ones. Malaysia is also home to the Batu Caves, which have 272 brightly coloured stairs to resemble a rainbow, which could very well light up your day as you climb up to the Sri Subramanya Swamy Hindu temple. Some Malaysian locals refer to it as their 'stairway to heaven,' and it could be my next challenge after my big climb to the Holy Monastery of the Great Meteora.

Climbing 280 steps up and down felt more like 280 just one way! The tour guide was in her fifties, and she inspired me by how she could do this daily. She even offered to go up, then come back and go up again to get me a walking stick. Going down is always easier than going up though.

As we were walking back down, I had a rare one-on-one chance to talk with Travis about the Bosnian Muslim side of things. It was probably one of the few moments where a Serbian and Albanian could talk peacefully about politics. I learnt why a lot of Bosniaks chose Turkey as a place of refuge, because it was one of the few places, they felt they could practice their religion in peace. I've also come across a

YouTube video called A Little Bosnia in Turkey. There's a little Turkish village where the Bosniaks have lived for over 130 years and keep preserving their own language and culture today.

I mentioned how things would've been better if the Bosniaks kept their agreement contract with the Serbians at the start of war. He mentioned that the pressure was also building up on them, after one politician stated that if all Bosniaks left there would be no Muslims left in Bosnia. Politicians are always the main cause of war amongst people.

Local house in Kalambaka.

Pinnacle setting.

The Big Staircase.

MIRJANA GLIGOREVIC

Three quarters of the way up.

View of the monestary across from me.

Edge Cliff

MY BALKAN HEART

Inside the Orthodox church.

Exterior icons.

On the edge of the mountain

MIRJANA GLIGOREVIC

The Tour - Day 10

Meteora - Gjirokastra, Albania (overnight in Tirana)

Hotel: Tirana International Hotel

We visited Gjirokastra, also known as the cobble city. I wonder why cobblestones are the main feature of many Ottoman structures? Like in many old towns, the cobble stones would be hard for people with a physical impairment who use assistive equipment to get across, but the taxi might get you reasonably close to the market.

Gjirokastra was the home of one of the Ottoman statesmen. I learnt who all four Ottoman statesmen were in Gjirokastra, and one of them was Serbian (Mehmed Paša Sokolović, the brother of an Orthodox priest who I will tell you more about later on). My parents had mentioned that the Turks ruled over our people for a long time, but travelling there really put into a greater perspective just what and how much of the world they used to occupy.

Not all classrooms have four walls. The world is your classroom when you travel.

> *"And then I realised ... adventure is the best way to learn."*
> Unknown

Gjirokastra is also the birthplace of the most famous Albanian writer, Ismail Kadare, who used his hometown in many stories. Up in the mountains you'll find the Gjirokastra Castle, also known as Argjiro, after a legendary Albanian princess. Local tales describe her as someone who lived in the 15th century and jumped off Gjirokastra Castle with her baby to avoid being caught by the Ottoman enemies.

It was another round of walking from one end of cobbled streets to the other for me until we got to the mountain point. My group mates went up for another big stair climb to get a city view, but I was too tired for more climbing at that point. I sat down and met with a beautiful friend instead. I never imagined meeting a real Kleopatra (named after the goddess). Her parents named her after the original Cleopatra because they liked how she was strong and powerful.

Kleopatra was only seventeen, but nicer than any teenager I've ever met. She wanted to be a model, but used to be slightly overweight and was bullied for it. She had lost the weight, but I didn't see why she couldn't become a plus size model either. Her words to me were, "*I could see it in your eyes.*"

She amazed me, and I wondered how she could literally see it in my eyes, almost like the real goddess! Was it some kind of super power, maybe? I didn't have to go up in the mountains to discover someone special, she came right down to me. It's my dream to find a life partner who can see it in my eyes as she did. Apparently, my eyes told her I'm a 'beautiful person who's been through a lot of hardship, but I don't let that get in my way.'

I figured out later that it meant she could see it in my soul (my walking when I'm exhausted), and eyes are the windows to your soul. Some empaths have the ability to absorb each other's energy, and they're the healers in this world. The briefest encounter with the right person can open a door or heal a wound. There are some people who could hear you speak a thousand words and still not understand you, and others who will understand you even without speaking a word.

> *"I found what I was yearning for—a mirror of myself in another person through the journey of life. I think I met my soul sister in Gjirokastra, and you might find her somewhere too by travelling far and wide."*
>
> Mirjana

> *"I know a beautiful soul when I feel one. The empath in me honours the authentic in you."*
>
> Kleopatra

As I was getting ready to go, the owner of the shop I was sitting in front of, an older lady, put on a friendly face and her palm down to show that I didn't have to go, I could just stay sitting. A very welcoming gesture for me. In Australia, I would sometimes get an unusual look if I sat in a café section but bought nothing from them.

A lot of Balkan grannies wear a little headscarf to cover their grey hairs, and it makes them look cute. It'd be interesting to see whether I'd be more like them, or like the French women who like to embrace old age. You probably won't deny growing old if you live to the fullest from a young age.

> *"Aging is an extraordinary process whereby you become the person you always should have been."*
>
> David Bowie
> https://blog.ioaging.org/aging/we-can-be-heroes-what-david-bowies-last-years-teach-us-about-aging-and-reinvention/

Kleopatra helped me over the cobbled road and up the step when I went to get a postcard of Albania. She said she would leave me in the hands of the other shop owner. I chose a postcard with Skanderbeg on purpose, as he's close to the hearts of many Serbian people.

The next shop owner then helped me across the road, where I sat down and had ice cream. My group soon came down, and I saw the mountain view captured on their cameras.

As we were leaving, Kleopatra ran up to me to quickly say goodbye. I had to take a photo with her, and I gave her a tight hug before I left. She told me on social media that night that she almost started crying during my goodbye hug. Don't just leave footprints where you go, leave heart prints too.

The group went for lunch afterwards. We went to a restaurant with a perfect name—Relax—just what we needed in that moment.

> *"Universe doesn't speak English, it speaks energy."*
>
> Mirjana

Kleopatra and I.

Gjirokastra souvenir shops.

The Tour - Day 11

Tirana

We went to Mother Teresa Square, where they have connected Albanian square tiles from all other Albanian countries (Macedonia, Greece, 'Kosovo').

> **Fact:**
> Albania is the only country with more of its people outside the country of origin than inside.

I had to stop and get a photo with the Skanderbeg Monument on Tirana Square. While Skanderbeg is the best-known sign of Albania, not all Albanians see him as their biggest hero. He was trying to separate Albania from the Ottomans for a while, and not every Albanian was happy with that. As the Ottoman powers started losing against the rest of the world, he became a bigger hero to more people. Meanwhile, there is a debate amongst the Serbian people that he was of Serbian origin.

Great 'Serbo-Greek' medieval hero—Đurađ Kastriot Skanderbeg—was born on May 6th 1405, on the Serbian Orthodox holiday of Đurđevdan. Đurađ's great-grandfather was a Serb from Kosovo, and his grandfather, Pavle (Παύλος), moved to Epirus (a territory shared by today's two countries—Greece and Albania). Đurađ's father was Serbian Prince Ivan Kastriot, and his mother was Vojislava Branković, granddaughter of Serbian hero from the Kosovo battle in 1389, Vuk Branković.

Skanderbeg gathered the Serbs, Greeks and Aromanians from the territories of the present-day Montenegro, Albania and Greece and organized them to fight against the Ottomans, who were helped by the local Albanian population. Named after Skandar (in today's Albania, but part of the former Serbian medieval empire), Skandarlija is the most popular street for dining and nightlife in Belgrade today.

The local guide took us through some bunkers from the times of their nasty communist system in the 70s, and I witnessed how the Albanians suffered a lot in that time. They had photos of the old soldiers inside the bunkers and it completely isolated their citizens from all other countries. Many feared death, and I really wonder why their dictator, Enver Hoxha, was so harsh on his citizens? Although the ideology behind communism is fairness and equality for all, it definitely doesn't always work like that. He made an angel out of our President Tito; no wonder Albania is the only European country which didn't attend Tito's funeral.

When the communist era ended in 1991, there were roughly three million people but only 3000 cars in the country. Some things other countries take for granted remain illegal today, such as riding a bicycle or planting a banana tree. We went to see the statues of some other well-known dictators, but the statue of Stalin in Tirana took me by surprise. I knew Serbia and Russia had good political relationships, but didn't expect it between Russia and Albania.

Aside from all the communist regime in Albania, the one thing that lit me up in Tirana was a great blend of colour to many city elements, which produced very uplifting street art.

When Edi Rama became mayor, he removed some illegal buildings and used his artistic skills to give the city a new lease on life. The end result was like a big man-made rainbow which added some bright vibes and helped me leave the time of their nasty communism behind.

> *"A rainbow is a symbol of how beauty can arise from or come after the darkest moments. Think of a rainbow coming the next time you hit rock bottom."*
>
> Mirjana

It also had lots of awesome commercials, and Tom and Jerry (one of my beloved childhood shows) on their post box was one of my favourites.

Although music theory was never my cup of tea, the musical notes made of stone and concrete lifted my spirits. You can change the rhythm of the world with the beat of love that comes from your heart. Inside the Tirana Park, below the green trees, was a beautiful big sign of the city's name. I took a photo with it as a representative of just another of my travel cities. While we were in the park, the young local tourism promoters went past in their traditional costumes at just the right time. Seeing a traditional costume of a country gives you a feel of authenticity—I had to take a photo with them. If you come across a doll in the national dress of the country you're visiting, that's a nice idea for an authentic souvenir.

Last, but not least, was our visit to the Japanese art installation, The Cloud Pavilion. It felt like a laboratory when we got inside, and I thought I'd discovered a scientist version of myself.

MY BALKAN HEART

Tirana Carousel.

With the statue of Skanderbeg.

Colourful street vibes

Colourful buildings.

With the locals of Tirana in their traditional costumes.

With the Tirana Park sign.

The Tour - Day 12

Tirana, Budva (sleep in Kotor)

Hotel: Hotel Splendido

What makes Montenegro unique? It's a country on the Adriatic coast, but with a Mediterranean climate.

You've surely heard about a white sand beach in Australia, maybe even a pink sand one in the Bahamas or Indonesia? But what about a red pebble one in Montenegro?

In between Tirana and Budva, we stopped to take a photo in front of the famous St Stefan Island. It is super expensive for an overnight stay or private getaway, but a hotspot for many celebrities. Some of the biggest celebrities have visited all-inclusive islands, including Elizabeth Taylor and Princess Margaret. It is also where Novak and Jelena Djokovic had their wedding.

The news about Serbs trying to prevent Kosovo's independence came on the radio. It made me happy, but Travis was laughing and I could sense he was making fun of it with his words in Albanian. He probably said, *"They're only dreaming!"* He probably used his knowledge of Albanian as an advantage in front of me as I couldn't understand the language. Even if you don't always understand the words with your ear, you may somewhat understand it with your heart.

The Malaysian brothers in my group used to work in a bank in Malaysia with some Australians, and I asked them if they thought I looked Australian? Travis said, *"No, more Serbian,"* but they revealed what makes me Australian on the inside. According to them, the way I say, *"Yeah!"* is very Australian.

MIRJANA GLIGOREVIC

I was so glad to hear that I'd caught a bit of Australianism from many years of living in Australia. It is interesting how different cultures perceive things differently though, for example, some tourists in Greece guessed my accent as British, but one of my British friends finally said what I wanted to hear—that my accent sounds like a mix of Australian and something else.

Many refer to Montenegro as the Pearl of the Mediterranean, and Budva is one of the oldest settlements in the Adriatic. While Kotor is the most popular place in Montenegro for the tourists, Budva is probably the popular spot for the locals.

Common travel advice from travellers:

> *"Listen to the locals, they know the best."*
> Mirjana

Geographical position dominates the Balkan region, and conflicts often occurred at the border between two sides. The old Budva walls were the line between West and East Christianity when the Roman Empire was dying and Constantinople/Istanbul became the New Rome, the religious capital. Many shootings happened on that spot.

One of the most important monuments is the big citadel fortress from where the walls start and finish. We walked along the ramparts and the citadel on the western side. I stopped in the middle of the Old Town and took a photo in front of the Orthodox Church of Holy Trinity with three bells and a dome. The design is like honey with red and white bricks from the outside. Dedicated to three Serbian Saints, it was built in 1797 with the approval of Austria after the fall of the Venetian Republic. You can't compare beauty on the outside to the beauty within though. The high tower of The Church of St. John (Catholic) dominates the town. Inside is a special icon called Madonna in Punta, or the Madonna of Budva, that the Croatian and Serbian people both worship.

The Old Town of Budva is on the peninsula of the Adriatic Sea and surrounded by so many beaches! I could describe the beach atmosphere as a relaxation oasis. It is where you would go for pure relaxation or a lazy weekend. Most beaches in Budva have so many banana lounges stacked next to each other that they cover the whole sand beach area. It's so easy to just fall asleep under the parasols and forget about everything else. No wonder the people of Montenegro have a reputation for being lazy. (I wish I'd remembered to bring it up or make a related joke about it during my time in Montenegro). They hold The Lazy Olympics annually, to see who can sleep the longest, and the people of Montenegro usually do well in it. If you are lazy too, it might just be your spirit place. Some of those slum parasols gave me a vibe of Africa too.

I was sad we didn't have time to walk along Mogren Beach, where you can get a top view of the entire Western Coast and Budva Riviera. When you go up to get a bird's eye view of any whole place, you feel you see the world in a way too. If you follow the path which leads to Mogren Beach, take your binoculars and find a beautiful ballerina on a rock. The Dancer of Budva is very sophisticated and adds elegance to the place. She points to the sky during the day and reaches for the stars at night. Remember—without the dark, there'd be no stars.

> *"And above all, watch with glittering eyes the whole world around you because the greatest secrets are always hidden in the most unlikely places."*
>
> Roald Dahl
> https://www.roalddahl.com/blog/2018/may/the-stories-behind-roald-dahls-quotes-magic

Other popular beaches are Jaz Beach, Slovenian Beach and Richard's Head (named after Richard Widmark, who made the film *The Long Ships* on the beach in the 1960s).

Our Budva tour guide was a very sweet blondie. The Malaysian guys liked her, and I regret not having taken a photo with her too. With a bit of spare time, I wandered through the narrow streets and into some souvenir shops. Some of those stone shops felt discreet from the big stone wall, but the treasures may also hide in the hardest to find places. When you get inside the doors, you feel like a local from back in the early days. What I found was great value for money. I got a water bottle which was big enough to last me for the rest of my tour, and a little beach box which said 'Montenegro.' It will be perfect to house the key to my memorabilia box from back home where I keep my cards and souvenirs.

No amount of money can bring back those moments you treasure unless you buy a souvenir. (Imagine yourself as an elderly person going through your life memorabilia box.)

> *"The goal is to die with memories, not dreams."*
>
> Mirjana

I had a late-night hotel dinner right along the Boka bay in Kotor that night. The full moon was shining amongst so many stars above, reflecting on the water below. The bay water was sparkling like the fairies turned it on. Only way to describe the atmosphere—Magic of Montenegro!!

> *Discover your life's purpose like it was written in the stars!*
>
> Mirjana

> *"We are all stars, but we must learn how to shine".*
>
> Marilyn Monroe
> https://www.pinterest.com.au/pin/5207355798719418/

MY BALKAN HEART

Budva walls from the outside

High city view.

Relaxing beach vibes.

MIRJANA GLIGOREVIC

Ballerina of Budva.

Inside the old walls.

Treasures inside the old walls.

Richard's Head Beach.

The Tour - Day 13

Kotor

The Boka (also known as the Bay of Kotor) is possibly the most beautiful bay in the world. I was taking in the beautiful view from the back of my hotel while having breakfast outside, and wished I had a room with a balcony where I could just step outside to the view directly.

When travellers hear the last name Karadzic, Radovan Karadzic (the former Bosnian Serb leader jailed for war crimes) is often the first person who comes to mind. One of the first things I asked the local Kotor tour guide was if he knew about the inventor of Serbian Cyrillic (Vuk [Wolf] Karadzic) and he replied, "Yes, of course!!" Not every school learnt about him though. While I know a lot of Serbian people who achieved great things go unnoticed, it felt so good to hear that someone was on the same page as me with history.

Many countries along the Adriatic are well known for their beach ports, which contributed to a lot of its rich history and economy. From 1185–371 Kotor remained one of the coastal towns that were a part of the Medieval Serbian state, under the management of dynasty Nemanjić. They named the town Kotor, and made a seaport which connected them with the west and brought great wealth.

We got into the old town walls through the main gate which the Venetians originally constructed, and where you might find their symbol of a lion. Traditional stone architecture is on every corner of the old town, and each building and monument tells a story. One of my first stops was at the famous clock tower. It's interesting how all the cities I've been to so far have one of these clocks. Bet you didn't know a Serbian monk invented the first known mechanical clock in Russia in 1404?!

While all the stone architecture looks relatively similar, they're each aligned to a different ruler, culture or era. In the old town's heart is the cathedral of St Tryphon, which is dedicated to the protector of the town and is one of the most important medieval structures. It reminded me of Notre Dame Cathedral in Paris.

You can sense the rich culture from the churches inside the walls. They include St Mary's Collegiate Church, St Pavle's church, and I had to stop and take a photo in front of the St Nicholas Orthodox church.

Arms Square is the main gathering place for the locals, and on the north end of the square is the Napoléon theatre. They sell a lot of souvenirs at the Old Town too, and many of the Orthodox souvenirs warmed my heart. The locals of Montenegro were even more heart-warming, one of the local stall holders in particular. Her friend came over with a little baby, to her surprise, and I can't recall seeing a bigger and more truthful expression of joy as when she said, "Hey ljubavi!" (Hey love!) to her friend's little baby. (It wasn't the English synonym for 'darling,' it was literally the word for the love between a man and a woman.) Her joy left a heart print on me too. These prints don't fade!

Happiness is contagious-
pass it on!

Mirjana

"*Sometimes, the smallest things take up the most room in your heart.*"

Winnie the Pooh
https://www.goodreads.com/quotes/1113253-sometimes-the-smallest-things-take-up-the-most-room-in

I was looking for the toilet afterwards, and asked local stall holders who were selling the cross necklaces if I had to buy anything before using it? They said, "You might as well buy a coffee for next to nothing, when it'll cost you to go to the toilet without it, anyway." That was another humbling moment from my people. Montenegro was where I came across some of the friendliest people, and the pain of the split from Serbia really got to me.

As you travel more, you will also realise toilet signs and toilets differ in different parts of the world. In Kotor, they had a ladies' high-heel shoe photo on the door for the female toilets and a gent's shoe photo for the male toilets. I was scrolling through social media, and fortuitously came across a quirky toilet item design—the travel urinal tube for ladies!

https://geekyget.com/pro.../reusable-female-urination-device

It looks silly at first, but is a good alternative to those hole-in-the-ground toilets for girls who have balance problems when they need to squat, or people who prefer to pull by at the side of a road instead of using very dirty toilets.

Montenegro is a place of many trees. The oldest olive tree is 2,000 years old, but guess where you would find the oldest tree of all time? I felt special when the guide turned to me and said, "In your own backyard. It is the New Zealand (NZ) tree, 6,000 years old." From the sparkling waters to so many stone houses and the olive trees, Montenegro reminded me of another fairyland.

> *"Advice from a tree:*
> *Stay grounded*
> *Connect with your roots*
> *Turn over a new leaf*
> *Bend before you break*
> *Keep growing."*
>
> https://www.pinterest.com.au/pin/842525042761575338/

Balkans is the place for cat lovers. In Kotor you will find cats from all over the world, and don't miss out on the interesting cat museum if you're one of them. Doors were open to cats everywhere I went. Cats were a blessing to people of Eastern Europe during the old ages when rats spread disease amongst them, and you might come across a cat having a snooze or enjoying the sunshine in every corner. I saw cats where you wouldn't usually see them, including around the restaurant tables, and coming into shops. I recall one cat coming into my hotel during breakfast in Greece too.

MIRJANA GLIGOREVIC

After exiting the Kotor walls, I found the Folklore ensemble dancing the kolo (traditional Balkan dance) out front. They were dressed in their authentic, beautiful and traditionally made costumes and foot tapped in a circle to a very soft melody. It reminded me of the beauty and peace within my culture. It was nice to see that some parts of the real Serbian identity were saved—within the wall district at least.

That night my phone charger didn't work and I rang up the hotel reception to ask for help. The receptionist didn't know what to do, but I told him to come upstairs to my room and have a look for me. We got it fixed eventually. Not a bad effort from a lazy man!

It took us no longer than twenty minutes to get from Kotor (Montenegro) to Dubrovnik (Croatia) by ferry. Ferries don't always accommodate people with a disability well, but many big bus stations do. (Check on the internet before going.) Short distance makes travelling by bus from one Balkan country to another very convenient.

The last time I checked on Google maps, it was under two hours of driving by car (91km). That is far less kilometres than local travel from any state to another state in Australia. Melbourne to Sydney alone is 887km. Australia is amongst some of the widest countries in the world, and the country attractions are also very spread out. That's why a lot of girls in my *Girls Love Travel* Facebook group find it odd when someone asks, "Is seven days enough in Australia?" If you want to compare Australia to Europe, think of the distance from London to Moscow.

Another girl shared her story about how she was going on a road trip around Australia, from Airlie Beach in Queensland, and she turned right from the coast to where the arrow said 'UK.' After that they drove to where it said 'Serbia.'

MY BALKAN HEART

Beautiful breakfast view.

Entry Point of the old town.

Diocese of Kotor.

Kotor Clock Tower.

MIRJANA GLIGOREVIC

Kotor Architecture

In front of St Nicholas Church.

Kotor Bazaar

Cat of Kotor.

The Tour - Day 14

Tour of Dubrovnik

Hotel: Valamar Club Dubrovnik

Hello to the pearl of the Adriatic! We travelled along the coast in South Dalmatia, near the border of Montenegro.

Feeling the travel blues yet? Or for a better word, escape to the blues. The blue beaches of Dubrovnik are so surreal, just like from magazines, but not photoshopped.

> *"We dream in colours borrowed from the sea."*
>
> Unknown

Research shows that being in a blue place can be more beneficial than in a green place. Beach water is the only form of salt water that lowers high blood pressure.

We were on the land of 101 Dalmatians, but nothing beats the *Game of Throne's* Capital Kingdom. Although I'm part of the 2% of people who've never seen *Game of Thrones*, I imagine King's Landing to be a place where the chambers of gold and treasures unfold.

My group stopped for lunch at a restaurant just across the road from the beautiful blue beach.

Connection to nature is very beneficial, and places like this nourish our soul. A sea change or a tree change might just be what be what we need!

MIRJANA GLIGOREVIC

> *"Allow natures peace to flow into you.*
> *Nothing soothes the soul like a walk on the beach."*
>
> Mirjana

I'll be honest, I also started getting a case of beachitude from not going in for a swim every time I looked to the beach.

> **Beachitude (n):**
> When you start to feel grumpy and snarky because you miss the beach.

We had lunch together, and I chose Pljeskavica, the Croatian version of a burger schnitzel. We were sitting across from loud Croatian locals who seemed very patriotic. I sensed it's with those people that political discussions would end in conflicts.

Once we got to our hotel, the hall was very long and it felt like I went through one big maze to get to my room. You could say I thought they were just as complicated as the journey through the twelve metre walls of the Old Town. I'll remember Dubrovnik for having the best salami during breakfast though.

History

> *Dubrovnik was at the crossroads of another civilisation and culture, but served as a place of refuge to the Barbarians. When the Romans no longer wanted to fight for the Roman Empire, they hired the Barbarians.*

Dubrovnik was part of the Mediterranean cultural constellation, yet intimately connected to the Balkans; Catholic, yet surrounded by Islamic and Orthodox neighbours.

It makes you think, "How would the Balkans not be a place of such blood and trouble when it's surrounded by three seas and at the crossroads of many civilisations?"

Dubrovnik became a trade centre of the Roman Empire, and the guide talked about how the people of Dubrovnik used to steal from the Venetians to make themselves rich. Back in those days, it was brother against brother in the fight for the emperor's title. They also used some tactics to save themselves from the Ottoman Empire (after they stopped in Bosnia). Dubrovnik locals were often trade dealers between the East and West, and you will find the remains of both inside the old Dubrovnik walls. The women often stayed home and suffered while the men set sailing. I remember hearing that Dubrovnik is where life insurance for women originated. Over time, they built a strong bond with the Austro-Hungarians.

Attractions:

- Dubrovnik - Old Town - UNESCO Heritage site.
- Large Onofrio's Fountain.
- Sponza Palace.

Three new ladies from Canada joined our group. The day's mission was the Old Town and our first major stop inside the walls was at the Large Onofrio Fountain.

In the Loggia Square I saw many important buildings—including Sponza Palace, the Loggia, and Gran Guardia Palace. One of the most interesting was the Rector's Palace. Sponza Palace and the Rector's Palace were the only ones that survived a devastating earthquake in 1667.

I thought it would've been even more interesting if we had the man who still lives in those walls as our tour guide, but the one thing that surprised me about my tour guide was how little he touched on the conflict between the Serbians and Croatians.

His last few sentences were:
"We're seen as these bloody people on tv but..."
"...and then the Serbians..."

I asked if we could go out onto the port at the end and he took us a step further to discover more. Always ask questions—you never know where they might lead you.

MIRJANA GLIGOREVIC

> *"Still round the corner there may wait, a new road or a secret gate."*
>
> J.R.R. Tolkien
> https://www.brainyquote.com/quotes/j_r_r_tolkien_132427

I was hoping to catch the island view that's always advertised for Dubrovnik, but I had to take a boat or catch a flying fox to the Srdj hill for that. If we'd had more time, I would've gone up the Walk of Shame stairs (a very interesting name) to find the Buza Bar, also known as a hidden paradise. On the enchanting cliff, I would enjoy the sun amongst the turquoise waters. That's one way in which Dubrovnik didn't fulfill my expectations, but don't let your unfulfilled expectations ruin it for all other experiences to come.

With a bit of spare time left to explore the Old Town on my own, I found a candy store that looked like a pirate's chest. I felt like I'd gone inside a treasure box and got a bag of candy from it.

Along the Stradun Street I came across a tall Dalmatian guy holding a Dubrovnik Heart of Happiness sign with some bells. He dressed like a boat driver and only had two teeth at the front, which was creepy.

I asked a Croatian local to take a photo of us and thanked him by saying, *"Hvala lijepo,"* with an ijekavica accent in case he was one of those very patriotic Croatians. I told him to hold my bag for me meanwhile (my purple bag looked fancy on the guy).

> **Travel Tip:**
>
> Don't miss out on the Dubrovnik City Walls tour if you're up for more physical adventures or accomplishments.
>
> Follow the route along the coastal ramparts through the medieval towers, battlements and fortresses as you like, and have a look out through open widows to some of the most amazing cityscape views. You might discover your own window to paradise.

They were selling some beautifully embroidered place mats, and I stopped and got Baba Stoya two little ones on my way out. The sellers heard me talking in the same language as them and asked where I was from, but not about my nationality. Bosnians, Serbians and Croatians may not still have the same identity, but they have the same feelings and bleed the same. A smile and a tear are the same in every language.

They were happy I got their product and gave me a blue bracelet in return. The first one they put on me didn't fit, so they gave me a bigger one. Once again, the stallholders were friendly and didn't ask about my nationality. I didn't see much difference between them and my own people. I think all the Slavic people still have less or more of the same characteristics and mentality. Every drop of love you give adds light to the world.

> *"World travellers are global citizens."*
> — Mirjana

Once in a while, you come across a work of art that touches your heart. Another traveller from Croatia shared with me this piece from her rental apartment in Zadar:

> *"All good to everyone, nothing bad to anyone"*

My first trip to Croatia was to Makarska in 2010 with family, and we had a good time. I think most places you travel to you will get by well if you go with an open mind and heart.

MIRJANA GLIGOREVIC

> *"My mission in life is not merely to survive,*
> *but to thrive and to do so with some*
> *passion, some compassion, some humor, and*
> *some style."*
>
> Maya Angelou
> https://www.goodreads.com/quotes/11877-my-mission-in-life-is-not-merely-to-survive-but

The beach scenery looked even more surreal from my bus window as I was leaving Dubrovnik the next day. Goodbye to Blue Heaven!

Stop in Neum (Bosnia)

> *It's interesting how you can't get from one end of Croatia to the other without passing a bit of Bosnia. You would think the little coastal stretch is a part of Croatia before you zoom in to the map, but it had less than more to do with the civil war between the two nations in the 90s.*

As part of our complicated history, the old Republic of Dubrovnik traded that part of Bosnia to the Ottomans so they could keep their autonomy (many, many years ago). That breaks a common misconception that Bosnia is all landlocked. People of Bosnia are very grateful they have somewhere to go out for a swim in the heat.

While Croatia has kept most of the beautiful beaches, the inner Balkan countries have other geographical features—lakes, mountains, waterfalls, etc.

Map of Bosnian Coastline.

On the Bosnian Coast.

MY BALKAN HEART

Bird's-eye view of the city.

Blue Scenery

In Strandun Street.

Inside the Dubrovnik Walls.

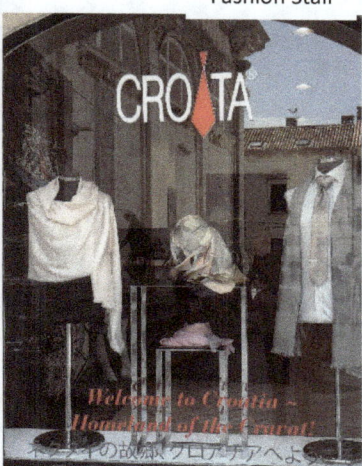

Fashion Stall

With a Dubrovnik local.

Dubrovnik Candy Shop.

On the Port.

The Tour - Day 15

Split

Hotel: Hotel Slavija

Split is another city which had a place in my parents' book of beautiful places, and I heard about its beauty many years ahead of my arrival.

The driver dropped us off right where we'd started our tour in Split.

The golf buggy saved us some energy (especially me) by transporting all our luggage to the hotel for us. It won't happen in many places, but if you can, I recommend you find out what you will have access to before travelling. A travel agent can find out many things for you, such as if a hotel has a lift or if you can buggy pull around a big hotel. Unlike with online bookings, they can also organise help with airport transfers on your behalf.

It was another beautiful place with one of the most beautiful beaches I've ever seen. Once again, I wish I'd stopped and gone for a swim!

> **To find out how the beaches in Croatia accommodate people with a disability visit:**
> https://blog.handiscover.com/content/tips-articles/what-to-do-in-tenerife/

While Croatia may be little land-wise on the world map, the beaches are the one thing they haven't lost. With so many stunning beaches, Croatia is a good example of how not every country's capital city is also the capital of its beauty, but Zagreb does have a unique Museum of Broken Relationships, a place where you can leave behind your old treasures from an unwanted ex. Great if you don't want to throw it out, but don't want to hold onto it either.

Other beaches:

> *Split: Bene Beach on Marjan Hill (with a ramp, toilette and special wheelchair for the water).*
> *Split: Znjan beach (with a ramp, lift, shower and toilette).*
> *Dubrovnik: Copacabana Beach.*

Our Split guide had a real love for her place, but my Canadian friends said she had to work hard if she wanted to beat their *Game of Thrones* tour from Dubrovnik.

Apart from the stunning beaches, Split is best known for Emperor Diocletian, who split East and West Christianity. That split was also the main cause of separation between the Catholic (West Roman) and Orthodox (East Roman) religions. They gradually enlarged the initial Roman province of Illyricum during a series of wars that brought much of the Dalmatian coast within their control.

Today's Slovenia and Croatia belonged to the Western Roman Empire, while present-day Serbia, Kosovo and Macedonia went to the Eastern Empire. It is interesting how many groups had a different influence on each civilisation, but they all lived so close.

Based on Croatia's troubled past, you would think the name Split refers to the split up from war, but nowhere does it have to do with the breaking up of the country. One theory is that it came from the Spanish word for palace - Spalato, while another is that it comes from the Greek word Aspalathos (yellow flower). The whole Balkan region comprises history, mystery and wonder.

After the collapse of the Western Rome Empire, the Eastern Rome Empire lasted for another thousand years before its time ended too. Some historians predict our society is also heading for a collapse like the Roman Empire.

> *"When you live in a false society, that bases its wealth upon money, then that society itself will collapse eventually. Not because I say so, because it's not based on physical reference."*
>
> Jacque Fresco
> https://www.inspiringquotes.us/author/7838-jacque-fresco

Our first major stop in the People's Square was the St Dominus Cathedral, which is the Emperor's mausoleum today.

Diocletian's Palace is a huge structure, with openings from many sides and built very strategically. I felt amazing when I got into the Vestibulum of Diocletian's Palace—rich, powerful, and closed-off to the rest of the world. The tall white structure resembled a castle.

The Gregory of Nin statue looked like a big wizard to me. He is known as one of Croatia's biggest national hero's for converting the Roman scriptures, which the Croatian people used to follow, into their own language. There were so many disagreements between so many historical leaders throughout history, but when different views were imposed on community is when the knives came out between the constituent groups.

Diocletian's Speech

> *As we explored the Peristyle Square, I went up to the balcony and had a photo of me taken where Diocletian made public speeches to his citizens.*

The tour guide asked me if I made a speech too. I just took a photo, but my speech would have been about how all people should live peacefully and get along.

> *"We were all humans until race disconnected us, religion separated us, politics divided us and wealth classified us."*
>
> Pravinee Hurbungs
> https://www.storytellingwithimpact.com/we-were-all-humans-until/

A humbling moment from Croatia was when one of the brides inside the palace said to our guide, "Cao Ana," (Hey Anna) from the top of the stairs where she stood, with the biggest wave and smile I ever saw.

Hotel Dinner

There were three tables outside set out in a triangular way, and I was in the middle. At one table sat a lesbian couple from the US, at the other sat a straight couple from NZ.

It was interesting to see the general differences between a straight and gay couple. I noticed the gay couple did a lot more talking and seemed more connected in their talk, but each couple was lovely and admiring their partner. You could tell they were both having a very good time on their kind of like dates. I was happy to witness that the gay couple weren't treated any differently in a place where many locals would frown upon homosexuality A single person's feeling of missing out when they're surrounded by happy couples kicked in for me. The couples made friends with each other and spoke about where they were from. The lesbians said NZ was their favourite country outside of home. After hearing America and NZ, I popped in and said I was from Australia. It felt like siblings had joined up together—America, Australia and NZ. Love wins!

I heard some loud music and screaming inside the Palace that night (in front of my hotel). It made me feel bad for others who live there. It would've probably helped if I had my Bose Headphones set-up to block out the noise, but it wasn't unmanageable. They must be big party people too. Crazy Croatia!

MY BALKAN HEART

Bird's-eye view of the city.

Sea view

Clock tower near Iron Gate.

Silver Gate

MIRJANA GLIGOREVIC

Emperor's Mausoleum

Diocletian's Speech stage.

Inside the Vestibulum of Diocletian's Palace.

The Tour - Day 16

Split, Mostar (sleep in Sarajevo)

Hotel: Astra Garni Hotel

I could say I was back at my doorstep at Mostar.

Mostar has become one of the most advertised travel spots, and I recall seeing it on many page covers. Prior to my visit, I had heard lots of positive reviews and about how it became one of the most popular places for travellers, but never had an opportunity to see it for myself until then. Hearing how so many other travellers come from the other side of the world to enjoy it, while I didn't even experience it in my homeland, made me jealous for sure! Mostar was part of what I had looked forward to the most from the whole trip. and for me, it was the most physically challenging part of the trip too. I felt like a little one who's just learning how to walk over those uneven cobble stones. I had no idea how the mothers were wheeling prams over them.

The local tour guide in Mostar, Jovana, was lovely. She had a first name that was more common with the Serbian people, but I think she was from a mixed marriage by the way she presented her story. I was very curious to find out about her combination, and people on the spectrum find it hard not to let their questions out.

However, it's taken as rude to ask people from mixed, war-torn backgrounds who they are, so I didn't ask her about her nationality. Curiosity killed the cat!

They would hardly ever say when they're mixed (e.g., half Serbian, half Croatian or half Serbian and half Bosnian). They would mostly say just one of those, and if you get mixed up it would get to them. It's known from many of the previous mixed marriages though that in most cases, if they have a Croatian father and Serbian mother, they'd say Croatian. If they have a Serbian father and a Croatian mother, the father is more likely to take on his wife's system too.

Mostar was one of those places where I also witnessed evidence of the sadness of war. We passed some buildings on the main street where the damage and the holes from shooting still haven't been refurbished. The locals had the Croatian army shooting them from one side and the Serbian one from the other, kind of like how my mum's town had the Croatian army from one side and the Bosnian from the other.

Apart from the music, embroidery is another mutual pride and specialty from all the Slavic nations that have broken up. In front of the market, I saw a lady holding a big, beautifully embroidered tablecloth. I would've loved to have gotten it for Baba Stoya, as I knew it was something she would love, but we didn't have time to stop, which made me sad. Doily place mats and hand-embroidered cloths are sold across many of the tourist stops. Many of them can crochet with one hand and produce some intricate designs. Traditional homes like to have them on many surfaces, on the tv, tv units, sofa, and so on.

Handmade is rare in Australia especially, and people appreciate the rare items. I remember that grandmas were often willing to give an extra dollar for the handmade items at the op shop where I used to volunteer in Australia. When computers first came out, everyone was looking forward to getting an email on the computer, but now people have a new appreciation for receiving hand-written postcards in the mail. That's why I sent many friends and family overseas a hand-written postcard. Some people say it's even more special to get something authentic from a country you'll probably never get to visit.

My cousin's five-year-old son in Bosnia was so amazed by a postcard I sent the family from Australia and it opened a new world for him, from handwriting to a geographical perspective.

"Where did the postcard come from?" he asked. The distance between Bosnia and Australia on the world globe intrigued him even more, and raised questions such as, "Did she have to come by plane?"

Opening children's curiosity about the world from a young age might be the key to success for those who intend travelling with kids later. They might not understand the value of some buildings if they don't know the history behind it, but the Great Wall of China is a good place to start. I recall a good first children's travel book called *Wherever the Wind Takes Me*, which my cousin read to me in primary school. Some child-friendly resorts offer good childcare activities or entertainment groups too. What a great way for parents to have a break from baby-sitting duties and housework!

Going to sleep in fresh bed sheets each night is a beautiful feeling.

The Ottomans shaped much of Bosnia into what it is today, and the people (especially Muslim) into who they are. Most Muslim women in Bosnia aren't as strict with the covering procedures as the women from the Middle East, but I saw some women in burkas (probably travellers). Mostar might have more Ottoman heritage than any other place in Bosnia, from the pavement to the buildings. I understood why a lot of travellers referred to Mostar as 'fairyland,' the unique houses and architecture of the Turkish have earned them a place in the history books. Jovana explained how everything was constructed with a special stone. Ottomans made their houses simple, but built smartly and high for access to good city views. Practicality on a budget was a big factor in the luxury homes too. Two or more generations often stayed in the same house and mortgages didn't exist.

How nice would it be if we lived in a mortgage free world?

There are limited ways for us to get out of mortgages today, but the trick to getting through life might just be having a holiday booked to look forward to. I also came across an article which showed that the happiest part of your vacation might not be what you think, but the pre-trip happiness. Cruises are great if you want to have all the inclusions provided under one roof.

> *"How in the hell could a man enjoy being awakened at 8:30 a.m. by an alarm clock, leap out of bed, dress, force-feed, shit, piss, brush teeth and hair, and fight traffic to get to a place where essentially you made lots of money for somebody else and were asked to be grateful for the opportunity to do so?"*
>
> Charles Bukovski
> https://www.goodreads.com/quotes/111168-how-in-the-hell-could-a-man-enjoy-being-awakened

We talked more about the lifestyle of the Ottomans and how they used to conquer the world. Travis mentioned that the Ottomans took one in ten Christian kids to their homes and taught them their way of life. The child would return to their original family ten years later and apply what they'd learnt.

The Christian population often served on the Ottoman conquered lands, and the Ottoman Empire wanted to keep increasing the number of soldiers to continue the conquest of their imperialism. The Turks often forcibly took the children away from their Christian parents, converted them to Islam and trained them to be the Janissary (the Turkish infantry) in a process called the Devşhirme system. Only the Christian children knew very well of their own suffering. It's something Travis didn't mention, and again reinforced how a lot of tourists take in the beauty without getting the full story of loss and suffering in many places where the Christians suffered. Sarajevo, my next location, really focuses on the suffering though.

Second Definition of Balkan:

Bal = honey, kan = blood, as in, "here you will obtain honey but this will require blood from you."

The destiny of the region has lived up to its name in many more years ahead.

Have you ever noticed how many other Slavic countries apart from Bosnia (Serbia, Croatia, Russia, Slovenia, Czech Republic and Slovakia) have the same colours and resembling flags?

It was defined at the Prague Slavic Congress of 1848:
- ❖ Red - blood shed during battles for freedom.
- ❖ White - peace and purity.
- ❖ Blue - honour.

Nevertheless, Bosnia shed just as much blood in those times.

Many Christian children didn't look back to their birth origin for many years, but there is one amazing story about a Serbian-born Ottoman leader called Mehmed Pasa Sokolović. Mehmed's brother, Makarije Sokolović, was one of the head Serbian Patriarchates, and Mehmed did whatever it took to keep the connection with his Christian family from the Western side after he came to power on the Ottoman side.

The bridge on Drina was the only ongoing source of connection between the West and East civilisation in those times. I heard that from many people, and came across Ivo Andric's Nobel Prize winning novel *The Bridge on the Drina*, which explains Sokolović's life and the events that paved the way for future wars. The bridge was destroyed by others and rebuilt under Mehmed Pasa's command. It was used to connect the Christians and the Ottomans, and is definitely on my 'to go' list for my next visit to Bosnia.

Sokolović's mother came across him after many years and recognized him by the birthmark on the back of his neck. He reminds me of a real-life Harry Potter. I believe he's still one of the biggest heroes to both Christian and Muslim people in his country today.

These generational upbringings from the Ottomans and their offspring caused conflict for many years ahead, and they split up the future Bosnian ethnicity (Serbians of Islamic faith) away from the Serbian Orthodox, who suffered even more from the Ottomans. Some Christian churches that survived the Ottoman emperors still preserve some of this evidence. Many historic wars also contributed to future wars, but the fierce battles in the Balkans go back thousands and thousands of years. Who knows when they will stop?

MIRJANA GLIGOREVIC

The Mostar bridge was the most challenging. I had to step on and over two levels of brick pavements each time to get to the other end. The ground structure wasn't convenient for anyone's gait (let alone mine), so I put each hand around each tour guide for support. I didn't fall, but my legs were still shaking due to a lack of balance.

> Don't wait until you've reached your goal to be proud of yourself.
> Be proud of
> *every step you take*
> towards reaching that goal.

"Mission accomplished in getting over the bridge!
Don't let anyone choose your path."

Mirjana

The bridge stood for 427 years before being destroyed in the 90's war. They fixed it more recently, and today it stands as a symbol of reconciliation between the Bosniak and Croatian people.

Jumping from the bridge is one of the most popular activities, but the Aussies have started going crazy for it too since seeing Hamish and Andy's jump on tv. However, jumping off a twenty-nine-metre-high bridge into the river is not something to take light-heartedly. You need to prepare for it very well, be a good swimmer, and have a cold shower beforehand to prevent hypothermia from the cold water of the Neretva River.

When we got to the other side of the market, the guide stopped us and told us to turn around and look at the sight of the bridge we had walked across. For me, it was a like a look back in my rear-view mirror to see how far I'd come and how many uneven stones I had crossed. Every one of those stones is a significant part of Mostar's rich history too.

> *"As much as it took me to find my feet in Mostar, the feeling of accomplishment was inevitable at the other end."*
>
> Mirjana

We ended the tour right at the Mehmed Pasa Mosque, just in time for prayer. My Malaysian friends used it for their prayer and I got to see some of their prayer rituals, including washing.

After the guided tour we were left in the riviera (pjaca) to explore. I took every opportunity to hold on to something, and even ended up tipping a souvenir off one of the stall tables.

I came across a lady, but wasn't sure whether she was a local or tourist, so I asked in English if she could lend me a helping hand. She couldn't understand English, so she called over a friend who could. I changed the language to local, then she was more than happy to lend me a hand, and said, "I can help."

As I was walking, I came across a local stallholder who wore a charismatic outfit of traditional Turkish dress. It was gold, and had a magical feel to it. I had to take a photo with her. I felt like I had met a real character from the movie *Aladdin* and I was in their world. The homeless boy from the movie was actually Prince Adi. A lot of locals from war-torn countries and people with a disability are a diamond in the rough like him. Those authentic Turkish tea sets on the market added to the charm too. Mostar as a place is a diamond in the rough too. At first sight, you see the tragic shots from the 90's war, but when I went into the bazaar those troubles from the 90s didn't cross my mind once.

Sometimes you have to look deep into things. You might see things in places you don't expect, but you might also not see things in places where you expect. Like Cambodia—it is one of the poorest countries in Asia, yet my work mate who's been there said she never saw begging, while the gypsies beg often in the Balkans.

Three quarters of the way on my self-guided walk, I sat down for a few minutes. Luckily, my Canadian friend came across me soon and I asked if she was happy to lend me a hand so I didn't keep losing balance over the cobble stones. She kindly put her hand up to help me and we got around to the Old Bridge for the second time.

> *"Kindness is loaning someone your strength, instead of reminding them of their weakness."*
>
> Andy Stanley
> https://twitter.com/andystanley/status/1039623383091216384

The bridge guys were waiting for the hat to fill up with money before they would do the jump. They jump for money from tourists as a way of earning a living. There are some very interesting and inventive ways that people find to make a living in this world!

> **To find out some more interesting ways that people make money around the world visit:**
>
> https://educateinspirechange.org/inspirational/striking-photos-captivate-what-work-looks-like-for-people-around-the-world/?fbclid=IwAR1uyaMOiDTssHIYa0zwXscar72-oTi2zKx3edSjuP0yF5wKIdMp7BxPbL4'

"How much does it cost for the jump?" I asked.

They jump for the tourists at 100 Euros and for their photo opportunities. There were many bystanders waiting for them to jump, but I didn't see many people put in the money. I was the one who kept on adding more money into the hat until I topped it up with coins. When three quarters of the hat was full, they said that was enough from me, but I didn't mind putting an extra bit in. The secret to happiness is to spend money on experiences instead of things, so why not?

What you pay for is what you get for adventures and experiences (most of the time).

> *Scientists from the Daily Health article said travelling makes us happier than any material wealth.*
> https://www.thehealthyarchive.com/2019/04/scientists-say-that-traveling-makes-us.html

> *"Travel requires an exchange beyond money. You take home memories and leave behind a bit of your heart.*
> *They say home is where the heart is... that is the curse of the wanderer. You are always home... you are never home."*
>
> — Andrew Bruzzi
> www.VendiumGlobal.com

It may result in temporary joy for some, but the happiness found in buying a new item rarely lasts longer than a few days and reduces over time, while the memories of your travel experience keep on releasing the happy hormone for a very long time. Adaptation is a contrast/enemy to happiness, but new travel always open doors for new adventures, discoveries and challenges. That's where travel and being open to new experiences play a big role in your happiness.

The bridge boys told me to go upstairs into the cubby house where I could relax and enjoy the best view. My Canadian friend asked if I would be right to go upstairs, before they told one of the other viewers at the bridge to take a step back for me so I could have the best viewing position at the bridge point. I thought I had to go up.

When the jumper saw me going up, he also came to take hold of my other arm. Inside the cubby house, they kindly offered me a cup of coffee. When the waitress told me to take a seat and then took the window frame off for me, I felt like royalty.

I was sad I had to go soon and didn't have time for the coffee too. Bosnian pride really kicked in for me as I watched the jump take place. On my way downstairs, I saw the jumper heading back up and gave him a nice pat on the back and said, *"Well done,"* for what he did.

> *"When I watch someone jump from the Mostar bridge successfully is when I most proudly call myself Bosnian."*
>
> — Mirjana

I realised later that not once did the ugly historic conflict from the 90s with the Serbians and Bosniaks cross my mind while I was in the Mostar Bazaar. The friendliness of the people in my country impressed me very much, especially in Mostar. In most former Yugoslav places so far, and across all three ethnicities, I could tell the kind actions of locals came from the heart. This experience will stay with me forever. I have heard from other tourists how nice and friendly the people from these areas are, but it wasn't until I visited my homeland with a tour group, as a 'tourist' from the other side, that I saw it in the bigger picture too. That's why I recommend for people to take a tour in their own homeland if they can and see it from the eyes of a tourist too, not just a local.

> **Travel Tip:**
> Visit getyourguide.com to find potentially suitable ways for you through Mostar.

When the tour members got together again, I asked the Malaysian brothers how they liked the Mehmed Pasa Mosque? It didn't meet their expectations—they said it was tiny. In their eyes, it was smaller than the ones in their hometown. The Pink Putra mosque in Malaysia, which sits on the edge of the Putrajaya's scenic lakes, is one of the prettiest and reminds me of Bled Castle on Lake Bled in Slovenia. Slovenia is the only former Yugoslav country I haven't been to so far, but the Lake Bled complex already looks like another place of fairy tales, just from looking at the photos.

According to what I read, out of the Balkan countries it has made the most effort to facilitate people with a disability by installing public phones with amplifiers, pedestrian crossings with beepers, Braille in maps at bus stops and more. I should also mention that Slovenia came in the top ten safest countries the last time I checked (despite the two-week war in the 90s) and is one of the cleanest and most hospitable countries in Europe. That's an example of how fast things can change.

MY BALKAN HEART

Rocky Road of Mostar Bazaar.

Ottoman houses and architecture.

Pathway across Mostar Bridge.

With the Mostar Bridge.

MIRJANA GLIGOREVIC

Going over the rocky cobblestones.

Preparing for the bridge jump.

With a Mostar local.

Jumping from the bridge.

The Tour - Day 17

Second Day in Sarajevo

For the first time during the whole tour, it got cold and I put on my long-sleeve shirt.

On some days, we must create our own sunshine.
    It was also probably the first time I noticed a major tan on my light skin. I felt unique and beautiful. It had been like a test to see how long it took me to get tanned—two weeks outdoors in summer, but I finally got it!
    The tan faded, but the memories will last forever.
    The tour guide was Edin Dzeko (a common Bosnian name). Most people who haven't been there just know Sarajevo for the gunshot that 'triggered' WW1 (referring to the assassination of Archduke Franz Ferdinand and his wife, Archduchess Sophie, on June 28, 1914).

Sarajevo

The word Sarajevo originated from Sara-jova, which means 'the land of the palace' in Turkish. Sarajevo used to be the second biggest Ottoman city after Istanbul.

Travis mentioned that the bazaar in Sarajevo extends from the one in Istanbul, which explains why you will find a lot of Ottoman traits in Sarajevo, although some say Saudi Arabia pays them to promote their religion. The hotel worker greeted my other group mate with, "Dobar dan," (good afternoon). It felt nice and cheeky to understand something another person didn't!

While the hotel worker helped me to my room, I used that time to talk a bit about his career. He'd been working for over thirty years, and I said it was very nice for him to have kept working throughout and after war. I said how many people were sad to leave their homelands, and I wouldn't have left Šamac either if it wasn't for the war.

From the Sarajevo hotel room that night, for the first time I heard an Imam sing, projected from the local mosque.

The local guide started by showing us street reminders of Gavrilo Princip and the place/bridge where WW1 was officially announced. It's interesting how it's called 'The Latin Bridge,' but is a Bosnian bridge. Many Serbs, including Gavrilo, wanted the people of Serbian origin to stop being under Austro-Hungarian authority. While many people think of Gavrilo Princip as the evil assassinator who led the entire world to war by killing the Austrian Archduke on his visit to Sarajevo, not everyone is convinced by it.

There is no 100% irrefutable evidence on either side, but there is evidence that everything was already set up for war before the assassination, the trouble was just waiting to happen. That's how my parents were taught at school, and even the English book *The Chronicle of War* states that the tensions between the great powers of Europe had been mounting prior to that event. It is a question of *who* rather than *how*. I could describe it as an athletics gunshot which marks the starting point of a race. Many believe if it hadn't been that shooter, somebody else would've started it. The countries later fought for their own empires.

The Serbian people didn't want to be under Austro-Hungarian rule. Although the Bosnian people were much more influenced by the Ottomans and the Austro-Hungarian's empire, not all disagreed with the Serbs about Gavrilo Princip initiating WW1. The Croatians preferred to be under the Austro-Hungarian Empire. To this day, the Serbians (descendants of the East Roman and then the Serbian Empire) rely on Russians for help, the Croatians (descendants of the Holy Roman Empire and then the Austro-Hungarian empire) on the Germans, and the Bosniaks (descendants of the Ottoman empire and then the Austro-Hungarian empire) on the Turkish. That is also the reason they're very split up on the opinion on Gavrilo Princip and the assassination of the Austrian Archduke.

We also went past the Archduke Ferdinand vehicle in front of one museum. It is a region that has been ruled by many differences and different empires throughout history, and at the end of WW1 higher authorities placed the three ethnicities together.

Edin, the local tour guide, explained a bit about the significance of the old Bosnian flag and kingdom. We also went to see the three different holy sites in the Jerusalem of Europe, including the Gazi Husrev-beg Mosque, the Catholic Cathedral of Jesus' Heart and The Nativity of the Theotokos Church.

We went to see the mosque and the Sarajevo clock tower first. The clock tower is believed to be the only one in the world that keeps lunar time, making it always seem like it is broken. Edin also explained about the similar time measures between the Jewish and Muslim people (both days start at sunset). It made sense why a lot of Jewish people sought refuge in Sarajevo during WW2, and why there is also a Jewish museum today. Some say Islam originated from Judaism.

I could say that my small Bosnian city of Šamac was also like a little Jerusalem, with different places of worship. The Orthodox church (Serbian) and the Catholic church (Croatian) were right across the road from each other, with the mosque located more on the side. I learnt how to distinguish between the three: Mosques usually have a minaret, Orthodox churches often have a domelike roof, and the Catholic ones have a rectangular tower structure. If you take a ride on Sarajevo's cable car, you might see the skyline of all three and many more attractions.

Next, we went to The Sacred Heart Catholic Cathedral. In front of the church they have the Sarajevo Roses, or red paintings, which the Bosniaks describe as blood scar concretes from the 1992 bomb explosion in front of the Catholic church. They were created by filling concrete scars from bombing with red resin. Locals sometimes turn symbols of pain into art afterwards as part of the healing process.

They established the Serbian Orthodox Church on the request of the Serbian Orthodox parish of Sarajevo between 1863 and 1868, but it fell under the Austria-Hungarian occupation in 1878.

MIRJANA GLIGOREVIC

Something else I found interesting was that even though Sarajevo wasn't the capital of Ex-Yugoslavia, it was still the place of Nobel Prize winners, including Nikola Tesla and Ivo Andric. There were more, but they are the two main ones I remember.

In the middle of our Sarajevo tour, we stopped at the East and West Compass sign paved on the footpath. When I turned to the west direction, I saw Austro-Hungarian influences. Turning to the east I saw the Grand Bazaar and the Turkish influences. It was time to explore the Ottoman side now. While many people know of Sarajevo as the place where 'East meets West,' I'm not 100% sure it always applies. The east part of Sarajevo has a little percentage of Serbs remaining today, but a lot of them have left as refugees since the war and the city is much more Islamic based. The Old Orthodox Church Museum in Sarajevo is a hidden jewel that can explain more about the old Serbian heritage.

Edin seemed very focused on the war crimes from the Serbian people and mentioned how the Serbs have taken away much of their history from the Old City Hall Museum. It made me understand why some Serbs lost the connection with Sarajevo, and I don't know if I can blame them for that.

To find peace, sometimes you even have to lose your connection with certain people, places and the things that create all the noise in your life. After showing him that I disagreed with some of his sayings later, it irritated Edin and made him have a think before bringing up how there's a statue Karadzic in the Serb Republic in a higher tone of voice. I shook my head on that and could've said more, but I had to stand my ground. He gave me the impression that all Bosniaks think that all Serbs support Karadzic. I wish it wasn't like that. Just because we want to maintain our own identity, that doesn't mean that all of us stand by Karadzic either. The big number of war victims who are described as Bosniak in the media aren't all Bosniak. There's been proof that some are Serbs too.

> *"We're Serbs. Everyone hates us for one reason or another."*
>
> Mirjana

Bosnia became a predominantly Muslim country, as Sarajevo became the second biggest Ottoman city after Istanbul. Again, it goes back to those Ottoman upbringings in Bosnia and how not losing their original identity was important for the Serbs who keep their Christian identity today. Many Christian Serbs agree that Bosniaks ignore who they really were and are trying to change historical facts. Christianity originated in the 1st century and Islam in the 7th century. It was all a very long time ago, but history arises in many future conflicts too.

   I pass many women who wear burkas and speak Bosnian in Australia today. For many Christian Serbs, it's a sad indication that those people have formed a closer bond to the people in the Middle East, rather than their original ancestors. Then again, it's hard to draw the line between freedom, respect and truth. The groups struggle to find the middle line. Despite such differences, I also sensed the Bosniaks feel much more attached to the old Bosnian flag than the current one with the triangle which represents all three groups. The Muslim people of Bosnia changed their identity name from Bosnian to Bosniak more recently to clear up who's who. Today, the word Bosnian refers to all people living in Bosnia, no matter what their ethnic group, even though we still have Bosnian Serbs, Bosnian Croats, and Bosnian Bosniaks.

> *"However dark it is, always find a ray of light."*
>
>   Mirjana

Every city has its bazaar, but only Sarajevo has The Grand Bazaar.

   The word bazaar comes from the Persian word bazar, which means 'market,' and I would've thought that's what it is too. It's interesting how they have turned all the original bazaars into tourist markets over time, but that's not original. The word bazaar originally referred to the central district of an ancient town, also known as 'the heart of the city.' As opposed to all the tragic traces of war, that was where I got a really uplifting vibe. The market stalls, music, and even the aromas couldn't help but lift my spirits. Walking through the heart of Sarajevo warmed my heart too.

Our first major stop within the heart was at the famous Ottoman Sebilj fountain in Pigeon Square. Lots of pigeons gather around the fountain, and I must mention it's probably not the best place for people with ornithophobia! I took a little drink from the fountain (believed to mean that I will return to Sarajevo again) and made the sign of peace in my photo, which also granted me a moment of peace. As we continued walking on from there, one stallholder took out the old Bosnian flag and told the tour guide to pass it on to one of my teammates (daj onoj djevojci). She got a free souvenir in Sarajevo. It must've been their statement of pride in the Bosniak culture.

I don't think you can pass through the market without indulging in your senses. My travel buddies described the traditionally made Turkish coffee from the bazaar as 'the best,' and I definitely recommend cevapi for food (minced meat sausages inside Turkish flatbread). The way they make cevapi differs from region to region, but the Bosnian cevapi are my favourite. Since visiting Sarajevo, I pick up on the smell of Turkish coffee inside my own home easier too. Out of all the Turkish inheritances I witnessed in Bosnia, I'm surprised I didn't come across one of their best-known foods, the kebab.

Most locals in Sarajevo are still very fresh with the troubles from the 90s obviously, twenty-five years on, but if you don't heal old wounds you will bleed on people who didn't cut you. I felt like the guide in Sarajevo had bled on me. It also helped to know this was my last leg of the two-week tour and home was coming up next. Anyway, when the time came to say goodbye to the tour guide, I used both hands to show him some warmth in our handshake. The way in which he went on about some things was very unpleasant, but I have some understanding too in him if that's how he was raised.

> "Love and compassion are necessities, not luxuries. Without them, humanity cannot survive."
> Dalai Lama XIV, The Art of Happiness
> https://www.brainyquote.com/quotes/dalai_lama_121172

Slovenes, Serbians and Croatians each speak their own language, but all three languages are remarkably similar. The Serbo-Croatian language was standardised during the Vienna Literary Agreement in 1850, following meetings with representatives of the three countries. When some local state people of Ex-Yugoslavia wanted their own country in 1992, they wanted their own language too, which led to more division. Many Bosniaks wanted to separate from the Serbs during the break-up of Yugoslavia, but many of them now frown on those Serbs who want to keep their own identity.

Today, everything in Bosnia has been split between the three ethnic groups—three official languages, three governments, and so on. The relationship between the three ethnicities might not improve as long as the schools and history classes keep creating divisions amongst the groups, unfortunately. It's complicated!

One of the things which has a positive impact is the teaching of Latin (the most commonly used writing dialect across the Former Yugoslav Nations) to Serbian children at school as well as Cyrillics (the traditional Orthodox dialect).

Acknowledging the Bosniaks, Bosnian Croats and Bosnian Serbs is a step forward in the reconciliation process, but a lot of it remains unresolved.

It has been my long-time goal to visit my country's capital city and I don't regret it, but I probably wouldn't come with a tour guide for the second time.

> *"It's better to cross the line and suffer the consequences than to just stare at the line for the rest of your life."*
>
> Paulo Coelho
> https://twitter.com/paulocoelho/status/998783036484390912?lang=en

The tour guide left us at the bazaar with a few tips on where we could enjoy the best food and drinks, but I was too busy shopping for souvenirs.

As I continued walking through the bazaar on my own, a reminder of my childhood innocence, and every other child's, came up. In front of me was a mother-to-be walking with her older daughter. They were talking about immunising the newborn when it comes out.

The big sister was a bit skeptical of the little one getting the needle.

The mother asked, "Why? The baby will be healthy after he/she gets the needle."

"*It will hurt the baby,*" the sister-to-be said.

"It will only hurt for a little bit, but will be all good then," the mother replied.

Unlike Mostar, Sarajevo is a much flatter city, which makes it easier for people with a physical disability to experience.

> **You'll find more information at:**
> https://www.getyourguide.com/discovery/sarajevo-l2281/wheelchair-accessible-tc239/?utm_force=0

I knew that coffee jezvas (mugs) are Bosnia's product of specialty, and Turkish coffee is one of the few things which all the Balkan countries proudly inherited from the Ottomans. I got Baba Stoya a special coffee mug for a gift. The art details on it are beautiful. I also went to buy my family Turkish coffee.

The shop didn't accept Euros, but the shop owner's friend offered to take me to the cash exchange station where I could get Marks. I went from one place to another and exchanged Marks the old-fashioned way. I travelled in an old time machine.

Who else remembers lining up at the post office when it was the only form of travel and communication? There was a time when our ancestors would come to town and just wait for their friend to arrive. They only used a paper map with a pen and referred to a piece of paper that had the name of their hotel on it. People made great photos with disposable film cameras and denied expensive phone calls. Who remembers working with their sixth sense for navigation in a new place?

Having heard that the Turkish coffee is the best in the Grand Bazaar, I regretted missing out on it.

By the time I got back to my hotel and met up with other members I could have probably squeezed in a quick cup of coffee. The only time I run is when I run out of money, but I don't regret it when I spend it on travel experiences.

Next time I will go to the Sunnyland theme park and have a little ride like the Olympians rode on their bobsleds in the 1974 Winter Olympics. If you like haunted places, the abandoned bobsled track might be the place for you instead. From my hometown, I would also take a day tour from my city to the bridge in Visegrad and learn about the historic significances from Ivo Andric's story.

MY BALKAN HEART

Sarajevo street view.

Gavrilo Princip Memoir.

MIRJANA GLIGOREVIC

Ivo Andric Commemorative.

Sarajevo Orthodox church.

MY BALKAN HEART

Where East Meets West.

Grand Bazaar copper display stalls.

In front of Sebilj fountain.

MIRJANA GLIGOREVIC

With Nikola Tesla in Sarajevo.

Along Mersed Berber Gallery and the Lunar Clock.

The Home Leg

Back at Baba Stoya's

Metanoia: 7 September 2018

> **Metanoia:**
> Origin: Greek
> The journey of changing one's mind, heart, self or way of life.

I didn't have to look for a home after the tour—I was already there. Soon after I went into Baba Stoya's home for the first time when I arrived in Serbia I felt under the family's wings.

It takes five men to make a house, but one woman to make it a home (especially in the Balkans).

I had home-made lunch with Baba Stoya and we talked a bit about life. Her old-fashioned kitchen stove reminded me of the closeness and warmth during meal times in the past too. Our grandmas often used to make propara (bread porridge) and it is still made in some Serbian homes today. The idea with the left-over traditional bread originated from the poorer households, but it tastes great when cooked and you add a bit of sour cream for flavour. (Think about how many Serbian kids grew up on it before throwing out bread next time.)

Our traditional housewife/homemaker always makes sure that the family is well fed before going out. She'd never let you leave the house without a full stomach! A lot of Serbian grandchildren would say their grandmas are the best cooks in town.

> **"I love you" also sounds like:**
> I made you this.
> Did you eat?
> Be safe.
> Call me when you get home.

"When the elderly die, a library is lost and volumes of wisdom and knowledge are gone."

Unknown

It's amazing how you can learn from and be inspired by the elderly. Baba Stoya mentioned how she'd been a widow for many years after losing her husband to cancer. It inspired me to see how she kept standing strong with no partner at seventy-five years of age. There's always something to be grateful for though. I remember watching a documentary on how a lot of women from the Himalayas go blind from the sun and struggle to get access to treatment, but Baba Stoya had experienced a very successful cataract operation to prevent blindness.

She's lived in a small flat for most of her life. I think when you hit a certain level of age and life experience you become permanently unimpressed by a lot of materialistic things though. Simplicity is the key to living a good life, I think. The richest man is not the one who owns the most, but the one who needs the least. Owning fewer things means less cleaning, burden or anxiety, and less stress every day. My experience in Serbia has reminded me I lost nothing by sleeping on a stretch-out couch, and I'm glad to have learnt it at a younger rather than older age.

I took up one of my cousin's bed during my stay, but they didn't mind sleeping together on another stretch out couch. Owning less is great. Wanting less is even better.

Love grows best in little houses, with fewer walls to separate. Where you eat and sleep so close together, you can't help but communicate.

Unknown

A satisfied life is better than a successful life, because we measure success by others, but we measure satisfaction by our own soul, mind and heart.

The other room (Baba Stoya's room) had a beautiful display cabinet full of her antique glassware (from cups, to wine bottles and flower vases) which she cherished very much. Once again, it reminded me of how the old people preserve the items close to their hearts instead of throwing them away.

To be rich doesn't mean to get everything you want, but to cherish and be content with what you have.

"Where there is too much, something is missing."

Leo Rosten

https://quotefancy.com/quote/1392452/Leo-Rosten-Where-there-is-too-much-something-is-missing

At times, our own light goes out and is rekindled by a spark from another person. Each one of us has cause to feel deep gratitude for those who light the flame within us.

Baba Stoya's next door neighbour, who used to be a kindergarten teacher, started painting her unit walls. It reminded me of when I went to kindergarten and our teachers would also draw and paint on the walls. I think there's often a connection between kindergarten teachers and artistic talent. One of my favourite ones was a painting of a prince and princess. The psychology of colours and how they can energise or brighten your day when you come back from a bad one is very interesting. Pictures have the power to open people's imaginations and bring the magic to life. It can be a very good learning and problem-solving tool for future learning, too.

> *"We reach home in many ways. Music, art, dessert, forest, sunrise, solitude.... Whatever revives the balance is what is essential. That is home."*
>
> Clarissa Pinkola Estes
> http://www.soundquest.co.uk/reconnecting/

She didn't always have enough paint supplies, but bought everything eventually. That tells me even though some people might live on a less than average income, they still invest in the little things that make their souls shine. Health does not always come from medicine, most of the time it comes from peace of mind, peace in the heart, and peace in the soul. It comes from laughter and love. Balance is the key in life, and you always have time for what you put first.

I think constant overwork and busy lifestyle have made the standards of wellbeing quiet low in Australia, and that people think it's normal to feel exhausted. If you don't pick a day for rest your body will. Respect your body when it's asking for a break. Respect your mind when it's seeking to rest. Honour yourself when you need a moment.

Nine Types of Rest (Author Unknown)
- Time away.
- Permission not to be helpful.
- Something 'unproductive.'
- Connection to art and nature.
- Solitude to recharge.
- A break from responsibility.
- Stillness to decompress.
- Safe place.
- Alone time at home.

Buying craft supplies and putting them to use are often two different things. I have a lot of blank scrapbook pages sitting at home. The power of art is often underrated.

In Australia it would be hard to get the government's approval for painting on these types of walls, which suggests that even though Serbia is poorer, it's freer in other ways.

I didn't know how much an artist could warm a person's heart before I came across an amazing picture. The most heart-warming piece of art I ever saw was of a girl in a wheelchair floating up in the sky. Demi, the artist, came up with an idea of someone floating, and then the exclusiveness from society for people in wheelchairs came to her mind.

I follow these happy sightseeings of travellers in a wheelchair:

Sonia's Travels:
https://www.facebook.com/onewheelticket

Ramped Up Adventures:
http://www.rampedupadventures.com/

You can find more specific wheelchair advice from those resources.
There are many similar pages you can follow on social media for inspiration.

MIRJANA GLIGOREVIC

For me, the picture represents a free-spirited girl, regardless of her condition. What comes out of art is amazing!
Demi (artist) is a young girl like me, who's also finished university recently. I believe the world has become all about profit, and the rich are getting richer while the poor are getting poorer. When you buy from a small business, you're not helping a C.E.O buy their third holiday home, you're helping a little girl get dance lessons, a little boy his team jersey, and mums and dads put food on the table. Shop local!

The craft markets with little stalls were also where I came across some of the best international foods during my travels.

Late afternoon I went for a little walk with Baba Stoya and got to see more of her neighbourhood. She took me to the nearest grocer's a few streets away and introduced me to the 'responsible rooster' who woke me up so often. We went past the tractor, the gardens again, and she introduced me to a few more locals—all the little things that reminded me that happiness comes in small packages.

I needed to get some female sanitary items for myself and the seller gave me advice on the best quality ones. That's the advantage of a small shop, the owner has had experience with the products, so she can advise you on the most efficient products for what you're after, even if that is just pointing out the juice with more flavour for a juicier taste. I spent 2000 dinars on candy products to take to Australia, along with some good female sanitary items. I heard from my friend that you should try Fanta in Europe, so I got that too.

Soon after we got back, Auntie Lila dropped by for a visit and a drink of coffee. She had just come from a neighbour's funeral, which reminded me of how lucky I am that I have not had to attend a funeral yet. That night I heard from Uncle Nick over the phone for the first time, even though the phone line was cutting out. I asked him how he liked his Australian boomerang and he made authentic Serbian jokes about how he would shoot Auntie Marie with it.

What I miss the most from my childhood is being able to walk in the middle of the road without worrying if I'll get hit by a car, and walking around the neighbourhood in the middle of the night without my parents worrying if something will happen to me.

Another memory I recall from my childhood—I was about five or six years old, and often used to walk to my grandpa's straight through a beautiful big flower field.

Many parents had one of those vintage cruiser bikes with a basket for groceries attached at the front or the back. They'd sometimes put their little one inside the basket too and drive them through town.

MIRJANA GLIGOREVIC

More Sightseeing

National Museum of Serbia

In the National Museum of Serbia, I discovered artistic, archaeological, numismatic (coins, paper money, tokens of currency etc.) and historical information from the Neolithic Period to WW2.

Vinča, Serbia, was amongst the first civilizations in the world. The culture stretched by the Danube to what is now Serbia, Romania, Bulgaria and the Republic of Macedonia.

I looked at the collection of monumental sculptures carved from quartz stone from 6300 to 5900 BC, and the archaeological remains from Lepenski Vir gave insight into settlements from the early Mesolithic and early Neolithic period, approximately 5900 BC to 5500 BC. I read the timeline about the rise of modern humans and the industrial revolution, but my cousin was less interested in that part. She was more interested in the information about how politics and religion evolved.

The Danube civilization (Vinča culture) was one of the most influential and important cultures in south-eastern Europe, and was amongst the first to develop copper tools, advanced architecture (including two-story houses), design and production of furniture, and a writing system. It's interesting how the Vinča survived without weapons, and while other parts of Europe were in the Stone Age, they were developing original ways of hand-making clothes and jewelry and more goods. The wives of the men who used to live up in the mountains grew needed plants and processed them for dying, weaving, leather processing and manufacturing to produce beautiful clothes and patterns. That's how they gained good hand skills.

It was so beautiful to see how some of those skills continue to get passed down to younger generations, and are all but a faded memory for some. Baba Stoya gave me some of her hand-crocheted cloths as a gift before I left for Australia. It'd be very nice to show and tell my kids about it in the future.

We came across a Chinese tourist in the money section while we were seeing what different currencies looked like in different eras. I talked with him about how the Serbian and Chinese people are good friends with a similar history in communism, and how I was glad he knew a bit about our country.

It was very impressive how well my cousin understood and spoke English with him, given that Chinese accents are sometimes hard to understand, especially in a foreign language. I said I wanted to meet and make friends from all over the world, so asked if we could be friends and stay in touch through Facebook. He reminded me that Facebook is illegal in China, and that's another thing most of the world takes for granted. I also read an online article about how the Chinese government is continuing with some extremely strict Orwellian practices for online use.

An article from BBC online, https://www.bbc.com/news/world-asia-china-50587098 , among others, said that from December 2019 citizens who want the Internet installed at home, or even on their smartphones, have had to undergo a facial recognition process to prove their identity. It might sound too controlling, but today being online is a bigger part of our lives than ever, so online safety is too. We rely on the Internet for so much—for building businesses and promoting them, relationships, socialising, and online dating for some. Sometimes it's hard to identify spams and hacks though.

> "We live in a world where there is more and more information, and less and less meaning."
>
> Jean Baudrillard
> https://www.goodreads.com/quotes/7834-we-live-in-a-world-where-there-is-more-and

I leant over to the glass a bit as we were watching the displays. The security alarm may have gone off.

A security guy came over and nicely told me to step back. When I told him I have a leg and balance problem he said he realised that, and was very nice about it. He told me I might hold on to the pole instead and said there were guys available to help me upstairs. I know awareness of people with a disability isn't as high in Serbia as it is in Australia, so my heart warmed when I saw how friendly and caring he was about it. Trust in others, helpful experiences, and allowing others to help you is important when you have a disability.

We went upstairs to discover the second section of the museum. They had some famous art pictures on display from the Obrenović dynasty upstairs, but I was hoping to discover more about the Karađorđjević dynasty too. It is a complicated story between the two, as they were always big rivals and often took turns in ruling the country. A lot of the Serbian arts and culture came to life under the Obrenović dynasty though.

In between the National Museum and Knez Mihailova Street, we went to see what variety of things they had at the Kalemegdan front market.

Maya saw that one of the fridge magnet souvenirs caught my eye and decided to get it for me. I felt bad and told her she didn't have to. She said, "I know I don't have to, but I want to," and the seller tried to give me an encouraging response with a Serbian Proverb, "Samo se umreti mora," (we'll only have to die eventually) but with a sense of humour and enthusiasm. Maya agreed to that. We also went into a souvenir shop in Knez Mihailova Street. I bought a small, authentic rakija (brandy) bottle. Now I have something to put the brandy in when going out and giving my Aussie friends a taste test. I chose the one with a plum (Šljiva), Šljivovica, as that is one of the most popular flavours and because growing plums is part of the Serbian tradition. A lot of tourists find it too strong and prefer the one with honey and a bit of a sweet element in it. On a separate note, I've learnt that North Serbia (Vojvodina) is the biggest producer of raspberries.

It was late at night, but Knez Mihailova Street was full-on with activity. There were break dancers on one side of the street, on the other so many friends/couples were waltzing under the moonlight to romantic Spanish music. I would've thought most of those people would be asleep by then, but Belgrade is the city that never sleeps. Not being locked in to a routine or having standardised times of what to do can be a great highlight of travel. City nightlife was another highlight for me, and it felt safer than Melbourne at night. Experiences in Belgrade also taught me just how much two of my home cities (Melbourne and Belgrade) have in common:

- ❖ Trams are iconic to both cities.
- ❖ Both cities are well known for nightlife and like to party.
- ❖ Both cities are big on coffee.

Skandarlija Entrance

My cousins asked if I'd been to Skandarlija? I said no, and they asked how I could've missed out on it?

It's in the top three must-dos in Belgrade. I was glad I got to experience Skandarlija in the last moments of my trip. They refer to the bohemian quarter of Skandarlija as 'the Montmartre of Belgrade' and many famous people have been there. It used to be an old and dirty street where poor poets and writers lived, but now is one of the most famous streets in Belgrade.

Don't underestimate amazing transformations of the big cities in the world. The Southbank in Brisbane, Australia, used to be an old wharf where all the prostitutes hung out, but is now one of the city's most outstanding beauty spots. Likewise, Dubai was a sand dune 1991, but became one of the most luxurious cities in the world by 2017.

Europe's first Kafana (a type of an inn) was built in Belgrade. Many restaurants in Skandarlija resemble a Kafana and have unusual names for a funnier vibe. These include My Hat, Two Deers, 3 Hats, etc. In fact, the literal translation of every Serbian suburb and city is very unusual to foreigners. Even I couldn't believe what the (very literal) translations in English were. The capital of Serbia, Belgrade (local: Beo-grad), translates literally to White City, but in English it's called Belgrade (not White city).

The locals are so used to it though, that to them they sound just like any other names. When a traveller said to one local that Serbia's second biggest city, Novi Sad, literally means New Now, he started laughing too. The country name Montenegro (Monte-negro) translates to Black Mountain, which some people would find offensive in today's age. We have Little River, Hungry Jacks, etc. in Australia too. So, I asked a Romanian person who used to live close to the border of Serbia and Romania how she saw the literal meanings, and how she felt about that name on the top right corner of the map below in particular (Serbian Nigger).

I find it funny because translations can get a misconception. Some translations are very hard, as one language might not have a word for something that exists in the other language, so they use another similar word or phrase, but it sounds strange.

Some people purposely translate something wrong, or slightly off, to make it sound funny. For example, in Hungarian, the informal word 'choke' refers to a kiss, and in Slovenian 'Ljubim Te' means I love you, but in Serbian those words translate to 'I kiss you.'

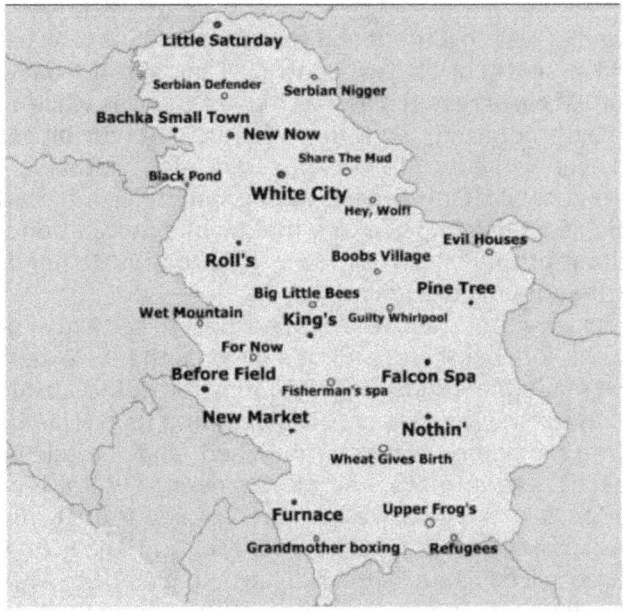

FOTO: REDDIT   Literal English town name translations

I was hoping we would have dinner in the Two Deers Restaurant, but it was full. As we were walking, about halfway up the street we came across a little performance with a lady dressed in fancy clothes, reading my soul out loud with a sing along with a man playing a harmonica (accordion). It almost sounded like opera to me. Maya knew she had to take a video of it, and she did.

Ponoc vec je prosla *vreme da se spije* *srce jos je budno* *davnu zelju krije* *ej, kraj pendzera stojim* *cekam da ti vrata otvorim.* *Zasto duso ne dodjes* *da me kuci povedes.*	*The stars are shining,* *The people are sleeping,* *My heart is pounding* *With joy…* *I'm looking out my window,* *Waiting for you to arrive.* *Why aren't you here yet?* *Take me to your home,* *Discover my heart,* *While I find my own.*

Skandarlija was so vibrant and full of nightlife, it took us ages to find a seat. Luckily, we spotted a couple in front of us leaving. Maya stayed to reserve the seats for us while I went to the bathroom with Jenny for make-up (that little bit of extra effort every girl puts into her appearance for photos).

Jenny asked if I minded her having something international and chose an Italian pasta dish that night. She can't afford to travel out of the Balkans, so I was glad to provide her with a taste of authenticity from home.

A tipsy waiter served us. I didn't expect to see a man be like that at his job, but it was part of a good, authentic experience and he made the atmosphere real fun. You get to absorb the crazy, awesome wonder of this planet and its people before you return home changed, enriched and broadened in perspective. I got to see a bit of 'Kafanska' sense of humour, as he focused on me since he knew I was a tourist from far away. I remember him asking me, "Do you know how the kangaroo got its name?" I said, "I have no idea."

He said that's what came out of an Aboriginal's mouth when they first saw a "kangaroo!!"

It was the second moment I got to experience a bit of compliments/affection from a guy, but I had to make a joke as he was an oldie for me. My cousins laughed at that. He said I should go to his apartment, where I would find out how old he really was!

Forget vodka, wine or beer it's rakija (brandy) in the Balkans! I got to taste a different rakija, one with a bit of sweetness and honey flavour, which I liked. So according to my people, rakija is the cure for everything—headaches, blood wounds, sore muscles, etc. It is also the one alcoholic drink you can get drunk and feel sick from, but you can't puke from.

While both of my nationalities are known for partying and drinking, I didn't inherit it from either! It wouldn't have been a real Serbian experience if I didn't take a drink of brandy on my last night and conclude with Živeli (a toast, like cheers!) That's exactly what I did!

I only drank a quarter of the brandy cup, so my cousins got extra. They divided the remaining in half and plunged it down their throats like nothing!

It makes me sad when I think about how I never had the opportunity to go out nightclubbing with friends sometimes (a highlight that many people associate with their young years), but this was probably the closest I got to it and the best party I've ever been on!

> *"Life is not a matter of holding good cards,*
> *but of playing a poor hand well."*
> Robert Louis Stevenson
> https://www.brainyquote.com/quotes/robert_louis_stevenson_205026

Second Last Day

I washed my hair and did some final fresh preparations for the long flight the next day. We went out into the nice sun to help my hair dry. We need to step outside sometimes, to get some air and remind ourselves of who we are and who we want to be.

I met the neighbours' kids and had a little talk to them. Once again, there were some humbling moments. Children in Serbia still find happiness in playing outside, such as playing hide and seek or climbing a tree. That's one of the advantages of not having access to electronic gadgets from such a young age.

I witnessed children enjoying moments of childhood without technology, as opposed to Australia, where it has all become about time in front of the screen.

There is an 'Addiction' sculpture in Amsterdam, a tourist attraction that brings to attention what the screen addiction that has taken over parts of the world looks like.

> *"Health does not always come from medicine. Most of the time it comes from peace of mind, peace in heart, peace in the soul. It comes from laughter and love."*
>
> Sadhguru

Many people aren't aware of the damaging impacts of excessive screen time, but when you're travelling with a person who has autism, some screen time is an exception. My tip is Bose headphones—they're a bit pricey online, but provide great help with sensory overload. I was probably the one who spent the most time on my mobile phone out of us, and I wanted a picture with the kittens the children played with. I also got to hold them and cuddle them. They had cute names with meanings behind them: Sinko (son), Zlatko (gold), and Bucko (chubby).

> *"Once we give up being attached to physical possessions, we find the time and freedom to follow bigger dreams."*
> Joshua Becker
> https://thrivingforfive.com/how-fully-commit-minimalism/

During holidays, a lot of children would go to the nearest school yard for recreational activities, and walking to and from school every day is still common in Serbia. In contrast, I saw a report on the news recently that said a lot of Australian parents get scared about being judged if their kids walk to school. Do you think we can we teach our current generation that a car is not a symbol of wealth, and walking doesn't mean poverty?

How Serbian Children Play

We spoke to the older brother about his school.

He told us his dad would reward him with an electric scooter if he got the best marks in all tests. It made me sad, as it reminded me there is still pressure from parents for kids to be on top of the class with everything. Saying that, he still seemed like a very satisfied kid.

I got a lot from him and Baba Stoya. Although you might think of those age groups as people who know little, or are deteriorating because of old age, it would surprise you to learn what knowledge and inspiration you can get out of them too (often something you forgot to think about).

There's a good show on ABC TV called *Old People's Home for 4 Year Olds,* where the little kids and the elderly interviewed each other. When one pair were asked, *"What makes you happy?"* the child replied, *"playing,"* while the elderly person said of the child, "seeing you every day."
(https://iview.abc.net.au/show/old-people-s-home-for-4-year-olds)

Young children give old people a new lease on life. A quick Internet search and you'll find reports showing how toddlers help the elderly living in aged care beat depression and loneliness, so make sure you visit your elders regularly. Some will drive miles to bury you, but won't even cross a street to come and support you while you're still alive.

Last Night in Belgrade

Auntie Lila knew it was my last night, so she called and invited me for coffee.

Just like the Serbian people would when they visit somebody's home, I took a bag of little essentials that fulfil the home—two bags of Turkish coffee and a chocolate for their son (although he's older than me). I'll always remember how visitors used to come over and bring me chocolate when I was little.

> *"The art of being happy lies in the power of extracting happiness from common things."*
> Henry Ward Beecher
> https://www.brainyquote.com/quotes/henry_ward_beecher_121522

She brought out some snacks for me and made me a big cup of Turkish coffee from her own place. The biscuit boxes were all unopened prior to my visit (probably saved for the guests). It's not uncommon for the mum to say, *"Leave it for when the guests come over."*

In our culture, the kids are raised not to touch what's been put out in front of the guests.

Even during meal gatherings, our housewife doesn't sit down until everyone else has finished eating first. Every time I tried to help with the dishes and chores at Baba Stoya's place my cousins would say, "Go and sit down please." In some places, everyone would be expected to serve for themselves, but in the Balkans the visitors receive the honours from the homeowner. Maya applauded me for travelling solo, and said she'd never be able to go to another country and culture solo (even at twenty-nine years of age). I think my homeland was just the starting point for me. I aspire to travel solo to more places in the future.

I knew my people were very hospitable, and had heard how locals from war-torn countries are more humble, but it was touring my country with a group of tourists from the other side of the world and seeing some things from the eyes of another long-distance traveller, together with them, that made me see it in a new light. I imagine many people who'd also go on a guided tour with other tourists in their original homelands and stay a few days might discover something from a different perspective too. Everywhere that I could speak and understand the language felt somewhat like home, actually.

I can also tell you that while there are still many divisions amongst the people in the Balkans, they all pull together very fast for some much-needed funds in times of crisis, such as natural disasters or life-saving surgery. The neighbours gathered and had a little chat on our way back. I thought the daughter of one neighbour had a disability like me, but she had sprained her ankle and was having a physio session the next day.

Last Day

Even before I fully woke up in the morning, I heard a song on tv which was reading my soul out loud again. That made me sadder, knowing I would leave then. I got a stomach rush when I first got up, like my body knew I was heading on a long flight. Baba Stoya offered to make me a warm cup of tea. Jenny would leave for work before I left to go to the airport, so she wouldn't be there to accompany me.

I made sure I gave her an extra big hug before I left.

As I was packing my gear to go back to Australia, Maya wrote a message in my book The Little Prince. "True friends are never apart. Maybe in distance, but never in heart. After all, the most wonderful places to be are in someone's thoughts, someone's prayers and in someone's heart."

I think when the dust settles, we will realize how very little we need, how much we actually have and the true value of human connection.

Stani Dušo Da Te Ispratim!! *Mesec zoru ispraca* *ljubav sprema se na put* *zadnju mi nadu odnosis* *sve je bilo uzalud.* *Zasto ides, srece ti* *nije valjda da si ljut* *mili Boze, zar je sve* *zar je bilo uzalud.* *Ref.* *Stani, duso, da te ispratim* *stani, preklinjem te ja* *zadnji put bih da te zagrlim* *zeljna sam te ostala?* *Stani ako srca imas ti* *na pragu umrecu ti ja* *bar mi zadnju zelju ispuni* *ja sam to zasluzila.*	*The last day has come,* *My darling is going.* *Give me a warm goodbye,* *For everything that's gone* *so fast.* *Do you have to go…* *Don't give me a reason.* *I can't believe how* *Fast it went.* *Ref.* *Wait another minute until I come,* *I'm begging you.* *Can I have another hug* *Before I start missing you?* *Wait another minute to* *show me your love,* *Or I will lose it at my doorstep.* *Do me one last favour,* *It's for my heart.*

I left something Australian for them before I left the house, a little boomerang each. They had an amazing reaction to it, like it was the best thing they ever saw in their lives. They really appreciated having something authentic from far away in their home and showed a big interest in learning about the ancient civilisations too. I know they'll take good care of it and cherish it forever.

> *"We are all visitors to this time, this place. We are just passing through. Our purpose here is to observe, to learn, to grow, to love... and then we return home."*
> — Australian Aboriginal Proverb
> https://indigenousworks.ca/en/resources/articles-reports/fire-and-dream

It made me sad too, and reminded me of how many people in Australia, and many other countries, still have little appreciation for their First Nations people.

I made sure the boomerangs were purely Aboriginal by the logo, design etc., but I know the markets also sell a lot of fake Aboriginal copies made from elsewhere. Aboriginal Australian is the world's oldest living continuing culture. Although it's a small population today at under one million, we have to keep embracing it for a positive future. If there is anyone who takes good care of our planet, it's the Indigenous people.

I was sadly watching on the tv about how the rich businesses have taken away many of their water resources. It broke my heart when I heard on the news how during 2019 illegal fires burned over 9000 square kilometres of the Amazon rainforest, home to the Amazon tribes. My *National Geographic* book states that jungles only cover 2% of the earth's surface, but are home to over 50% of all known living things.

Likewise, I felt in a catastrophic state when I read that ecologists from the University of Sydney, Australia, estimate that 480 million mammals, birds, and reptiles were killed in the 2019/20 bushfires. This includes 8,000 koalas, who are now near total extinction. It was the highest rate of loss on earth so far, and a question of how our ecosystem will survive. I cherish my photo with a koala very much, and encourage everyone to make the most of this beautiful planet before everything else goes too.

Not every country is equally rich financially, but not every country measures wealth the same way either. Bhutan measures wealth according to the wellbeing of their citizens. Australia's famous travel host, Catriona Rowntree, once stated that Bhutan was her favourite place she's ever been to because of its uniqueness. It's the only country in the world which never faced a water crisis, food crisis or any kind of pollution. In fact, it is the only carbon negative country in the world, as it absorbs more carbon dioxide than it produces. Wouldn't it be nice if the entire world was like Bhutan too?

> https://www.nationalgeographic.com/travel/destinations/asia/bhutan/carbon-negative-country-sustainability/

I've heard many travellers who've been to Scandinavia say it's one of the few places where nature is still somewhat untamed by the global warming crisis, and the locals live a great lifestyle too. The number of people riding a bike in Scandinavia will blow you away! Riding a bike is probably the next best way to experience a country after walking. You can see things better in open air and it's easier for many people to cover more kilometres, compared to walking.

I want to travel to places where the locals enjoy life and have fun.

According to the World Economic Forum organisation, the five happiest countries on earth (based on social support, good health care and freedom to live life how you choose) are Finland, Denmark, Norway, Iceland and Netherlands.

> https://www.weforum.org/agenda/2018/03/these-are-the-happiest-countries-in-the-world/

Another rare and impressive place I read about is Auroville, a city of India, where people live without politics, religion or money. It's not a place you would travel to for the scenery, but for the living ideals of people who do not follow the 'normal' society standards. While most of us live in a world based on greed and profit, those little places are where you can find peace still exists.

Often, it's the unique places travellers like the most. Some common favourites from well experienced travellers I spoke to were India, Jordan and Morocco.

> *"A big house is nice, but a roof over your head is more important."*
>
> Mirjana

Travel can open your eyes and mind and change you for the better in so many ways. People travel for many reasons. I heard from an international student from Mauritius that many people in his home country travel to cold Russia to appreciate their year-round warm weather. Life is so ironic. It takes sadness to know what happiness is, noise to appreciate silence, and absence to value presence. Even when travel teaches you something that you had an intention of learning or experiencing, it becomes a valuable life lesson.

A good life is a collection of happy moments. I make happy moments by travelling. To travel is to live the life I love wherever I go.

> *"If you have food in the refrigerator, clothes on your back, a roof over your head, and a place to sleep, you are richer than 75% of the world."*
>
> Wayne Dyer
> http://famousquotefrom.com/wayne-dyer/

MY BALKAN HEART

Paintings

Walking on residential street.

MIRJANA GLIGOREVIC

Mother statue in Motherland. (At the National Museum in Serbia.)

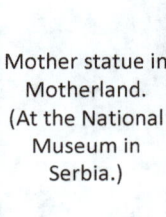

Museum image that shows generational suffering.

Big Ottoman earings on display.

MY BALKAN HEART

Night show.

Final toast with my cousins.

How guests get served (at Aunt Lila's).

MIRJANA GLIGOREVIC

Wonderland

The mother of the girl with a sprained ankle came to Baba Stoya's for a coffee on my last day too. Guests coming over for a coffee and chat is a regular part of their lifestyle, like in many other Serbian homes.

"*Come over for coffee,*" refers to coming over for a chill and chat in my culture.

I was packing my bags and we were talking about leaving. She only saw me for the second time, but was so friendly it was like I was a very close friend of hers. She wished me safe travels before she left (*Sretan Put Mirjana*).

Baba Stoya gave me her handmade cloths as a gift from her. I will surely put them on my home surfaces to make the house warmer, like in Serbia.

I left 500 dinars for each person in the house before I left, so they could get themselves a little something, and paid the rest for Uncle Mick's drive back to the airport. I asked him was that enough? He made a little joke that it's enough for a bottle of beer with his brother-in-law. I also took a special rakija bottle, a present from Uncle Nick to my dad. It was a homemade family brand and came in a special bottle that had our family name on it.

An Anonymous Journalist on Serbia

I've travelled the whole world, but this country is phenomenal:
- ❖ The country that has a borderline with its own self.
- ❖ Where the most beautiful women live, but the birth rate declines.
- ❖ Where the unemployed work the most; where the hungry live on the most fertile land.
- ❖ Where the trains run later than cars.
- ❖ Where everyone plays soccer, but wins in water polo, basketball and tennis.
- ❖ Where everyone rushes to work and no one arrives on time.
- ❖ Where the 8 hour opening hours are 12 hours.
- ❖ Where healthcare is free and treatment is expensive.
- ❖ Where journalists are free to write whatever they are ordered to do.
- ❖ Where the world crisis got its citizenship.
- ❖ Where public procurement is secret and state secrets are public.
- ❖ Where wars never end.
- ❖ Where history repeats itself every day.
- ❖ Where the richest ones are those who have never worked.
- ❖ Where foreign currency is exchanged for domestic currency.
- ❖ Where people celebrate their Patron Saint Day but curse God.
- ❖ Where laws are illegal and anarchy is accepted.
- ❖ Where the authorities despise citizens as unwanted witnesses.
- ❖ Where people depend on the future because they are not entitled to the present.
- ❖ Where everyone smiles at everyone, and nobody wishes anyone well. (Although I would say it can be the opposite too.)
- ❖ Where court proceedings last longer than life.
- ❖ Where floods are a way of watering the land.
- ❖ Where they think the country will prosper more if they decline more.
- ❖ Where you're not normal if you don't go crazy.
- ❖ Where you live only to die, where time is infinite and power is immortal.

MIRJANA GLIGOREVIC

> *"Alice doesn't know what Wonderland is.*
> *She's never been to Serbia."*
>
> — Mirjana

Auntie Lila had left work early to escort me to the airport. A hospitable Serb would never let you leave their yard without escorting you. If there is one day they would take off work, it would be to await and accompany the guest.

My cousin's last few words to me were, *"Come again soon."* I told her I intended on travelling the world on a wider scale now, but that I would pop by if I ever went past Belgrade again. Serbia shares a border with six other countries (seven if you include Kosovo), but so many travellers just go around it.

Travel researchers found that eight days is just the right time to recharge your batteries when going on a holiday or vacation.

> https://www.inc.com/jessica-stillman/science-says-this-is-the-ideal-vacation-length.html

The article also shows that those who constantly focus on work and earning money are less likely to relax and enjoy it. Life is not just about how much you're earning—life is about how you're living it. You often feel tired not because you did too much, but because you've done too little of what sparks a light in you. I was watching Lacey Filipich, who travelled with two kids and invested in herself, on Australia's *The Daily Show*. The thirty-one-year-old released a book called *Money School* to help others invest more in themselves too.

It's not just about the length of life, but the depth of life too. I believe travel is a big factor in living life to the fullest, and that is one reason I wrote this book to inspire people.

> *"Destroy the idea that you have to be constantly working or grinding in order to be successful. Embrace the concept that rest, recovery, reflection are essential parts of the progress towards a successful and happy life."*
>
> — Zach Galifianakis
>
> https://ifunny.co/picture/destroy-the-idea-that-you-have-to-be-constantly-working-mMqM1BoQ6

MY BALKAN HEART

Research by Booking.com also reported it doesn't matter if you're a backpacker or stay at a luxurious hotel, every travel experience increases endorphins and positively affects your health. For many people who value travelling highly, it also outweighs other events such as getting married, having a kid, and tops the list of things that bring the most joy to life.

I met a guy once on a flight to Thailand who started travelling the world as a way of coping with some of his problems. He said he hadn't looked back since, and that travel gives you a good opportunity to start afresh in a new place with different people. Likewise, I've talked to many people who say they found healing in travel too, whether it's healing from a breakup, the loss of a loved one, or Post Traumatic Stress Disorder.

I regret nothing from my time in Serbia. I just wish I had visited the White Royal Palace, too. It will be the first thing on my to-do list in Serbia next time, or I might even take a day trip from Bosnia to the White Palace. I might've even been lucky enough to meet with Serbia's 'Royal' family. The Palace deserves more recognition, but isn't as well advertised as some other attractions in Belgrade.

Serbia's Royal History will melt your heart, especially with the last few generations. It even touched Prince Charles when he looked into the family's history on his visit to the White Palace in 2016.

Most Serbs know of Prince Peter II of Yugoslavia's sad history, and I feel bad about the big generational gaps between the great-grandfather, grandfather, the last hereditary little prince and his son (Prince Alexander Karadjordjević). Although Prince Peter II of Yugoslavia lost his title at such a young age and had to flee from home, living in Britain for most of his life, his son spoke in a public interview about how his father always expressed the wish to finally rest with all his other ancestors. That goes to show how even though you might go in a different direction, your family origin will always remain at the back of your head.

I'm very glad about recent changes with the federal law of Serbia which allowed it to happen. Crown Prince Alexander's biggest 'royal' achievement was probably when he had a decent number of Serbian citizens following him at his father's funeral in Serbia. Although the family hasn't been given their

MIRJANA GLIGOREVIC

royal title back, they still do a lot of humanitarian work and good deeds for their country, like most other royals would for their country.

According to the tour guide of the Victorian Parliament Building in Australia, royal privileges are decreasing today in most other monarchy countries too, compared to the older generations, but I'd like to see his son Prince Alexander receive at least some royal honours in his lifetime. The former Socialist Republic of Ex-Yugoslavia was good under Tito's rule, but those days are long gone. The middle son of Prince Alexander has made a promise to the Serbian Patriarch that his little son will grow up in Serbia. While the Karađjorđjević family are safely back home today, only time will tell if they will ever be the official monarchy again. LONG LIVE THE KING!!!

I also wish I gave more back to the Serbian refugees who weren't lucky enough to live a better life elsewhere. Another *Girls Love Travel* member directed a group mate to a great volunteering opportunity in Belgrade that she had experienced. It used to be BelgrAID and is now Collective Aid. Collective Aid is based in Serbia, but helps a lot of refugees from Serbia and throughout the whole Balkan region. A lot of the coordinators aren't Serbian themselves. They provide cooked meals, free aid and social activities for the refugees. Even a few hours of volunteering will make a big difference. You'll meet people, their life stories will touch you, and you can do your part for the local community. A small place could take up a big place in your heart.

> **To get involved go to:**
> https://www.collectiveaidngo.org/ways-to-help-landing
>
> *Girls Love Travel* is a global Facebook community page which shares great resources, advice and empowerment to girls who intend travelling. It might just give you that extra bit of support you need to push you over the edge for your next trip.

Travel can also be a great way to do your part for the less fortunate communities in the world, as long as you do it ethically. Organisations such as Contiki and G-Adventures often provide things that incorporate local benefits. Reach Out Volunteers has a good range of fundraising projects and you can choose based on your own passion. One of my friends went on a voluntary mission to Africa with Reach Out and took part in building a creche and a first aid clinic and went to a few animal sanctuaries. She said it was one of her best life experiences.

For more volunteering information on a bigger world scale visit:

https://www.rovolunteers.com/?gclid=Cj0KCQjw1Iv0BRD aARIsAGTWD1uiS144_rrWSgYKpzPPxbJD9_t1NjKf01ccAav TF47i_nNHivxOl2caAnIfEALw_wcB

> *"When you choose joy, you feel good, and when you feel good, you do good, and when you do good it reminds others of what joy feels like and it just might inspire them to do the same."*
>
> Author Unknown
> https://theweeklysparkle.com/tag/how-to-feel-joy/

Serbia's second biggest city, Novi Sad, is also worth a visit. It is like Belgrade, but with a more laid-back vibe. The name Novi Sad (New Now) reflects the city for what it is—multicultural, with lots of beautiful cathedrals, Petrovaradin Fortress, pools, shopping etc.

> **Did You Know...**
>
> Novi Sad was the home of Albert Einstein and his first wife, Mileva Maric, a Serbian female figure who didn't get enough credit for her fantastic achievements. If you pass the building Kisacka 21 in Novi Sad, you'll see where the couple spent their spare time with friends and played music.
>
> Learn more about the interesting life of his first wife at:
>
> https://blogs.scientificamerican.com/guest-blog/the-forgotten-life-of-einsteins-first-wife/?fbclid=IwAR2Ehk99NLPg1gGD5D_eAeKwHc-aH-hS2bulRDzBv5UqXUKvKh6TYLY_wfc

MIRJANA GLIGOREVIC

Homecoming

> "Why do you go away? So that you can come back. So that you can see the place you came from with new eyes and extra colours. And the people there see you differently, too. Coming back to where you started is not the same as never leaving."
>
> Terry Pratchett
> https://www.goodreads.com/quotes/67857-why-do-you-go-away-so-that-you-can-come

When you spend some time in a place/region that's more corrupt than where you live, part of the happiness is knowing that you'll return to your other home soon too. A part of me and my pride will always remain in my country of origin, but I still think Australia is one of the best countries to live in. Many people who haven't travelled much out of Australia probably don't realise how lucky they are.

People who leave their homeland are often pulled to go back and visit on a regular basis too.

As I got into the passenger zone at the airport, I was hoping to come across that rare alphabet book (azbuka) from my generation with the blue bird at the cover page. I asked the book seller and he did take out an azbuka, but it wasn't the version I had hoped for.

I was also looking forward to going into the Novak Djokovic shop that had opened in 2016 to buy one of his unique tennis balls, but unfortunately for me it had closed very soon after opening. After many years of research on how to prevent muscle numbness on long flights, London Orthopedic Surgeon, Ali Gjoz, suggests using a tennis ball.

https://www.travelandleisure.com/airlines-airports/tennis-ball-travel-tip

It's very convenient and easy to carry in your handbag too. Rolling a tennis ball on different muscle points is equivalent to a massage and stretching the muscles, which regulates a good blood flow. Compression socks are also highly recommended for people with numbness problems (it often includes people with Cerebral Palsy). I usually book the aisle seat on long flights so I can stand up and take a walk on a regular basis. I was impressed with the amount of seat and leg space on Air Serbia though.

Most people at the airport know what's it like to be on a long flight and the place is made to cater for everyone. One of the great things for anyone, especially people with a disability, is that the social rules of society don't apply at an airport. You can dress however you feel comfortable, eat and drink at whatever time you want and sleep wherever you get a chance. I have witnessed rows of people sleeping by the wall in the airport hallway on my return to Melbourne at five in the morning. Even if you can't sleep in your own bed at 2am and you just want to get out, you can go to the airport and watch plane departures or landings.

Jenny had given me a little colouring book and a mini colouring pencils pack as a gift, which served me well on my long flight. On the plane to Rome, I saw a few fancy-dressed Italians in costumes. One man was wearing a big hat, like a magician's one. I could tell they were Italian. There was a little blonde boy with his mum who was especially cute while blocking his nose during the take-off. I heard them talking another language and wondered what it was.

I asked them in English first, but the boy tapped to his mum and they were both looking at me with confusion. I then changed to International words: Turkish? Romanian?

The boy then answered, "*Italian*" (the European way).

MIRJANA GLIGOREVIC

> *"Welcome Serbian.*
> *-Dress Italian.*
> *-Kiss French.*
> *Travel to see what you should pick up from each country.*
> *All roads lead to Rome... (and here I am).*
> *Coincidence??"*
>
> Mirjana

I never thought I'd end-up in Rome like that, but never say never. When I first learnt that my stopover from Serbia would be in Rome for a few hours I was so excited and went on Google Maps to see how far the airport was from the Trevi Fountain. I considered catching a taxi to go and throw a coin in the fountain, but unfortunately time at the airport between when you check in and check out goes fast!

We got straight on the airport train to the check in point. An airport is one of the very few places where you can't get lost if you follow the crowd. I tried to use some basic Italian words with the airport staff, pulling on what I remembered from learning Italian at school, such as ciao, grazie etc. I wished I knew more Italian at that point! Learning the manners and the basics of any country you visit probably goes a long way though.

I was going through my plane tickets when a flight attendant said with a charming smile, *"You look like you're on a long trip."* My next stop was Abu Dhabi again. One of the flight attendants saw my language tag peeking out of the cabins, pointed to it, and asked if I was Serbian. I said, *"Yes,"* and she replied, *"Mi smo iste,"* which means 'we're our own.'

Although I have autism, I still like to stop by and engage in these types of social conversations every now and then. For example, I find it hard to just walk by without stopping to introduce myself when I hear someone speak the same language. There's probably still less or more of that in us (Eastern Europeans), although I watched a video interview from a middle-aged Balkan man who lives 'an old lifestyle' up in the mountains and is trying very hard to raise his kids the way his grandpa raised him.

His grandpa knew that we'd live in a terrible society if/when profit takes over and people lose the family connection with each other. When asked about his perspective on life and what he thinks men have lost in today's age, he said, "Lots—understanding, respect, an interest in other people. When two acquaintances pass by each other, they hardly ever stop just to say hi these days." That's why he thinks many kids have trouble finding themselves in today's civilisation, however he still believes that things like respect and trust will come out on top eventually (at least in his society).

Just across from me were a boyfriend and girlfriend couple. They guy had a flu, and the flight attendant gave him some Panadol. Flight attendants are usually lovely and can assist with anything from holding a baby while the mother gets into a comfortable position, to helping you exit the plane. The guy had his mouth covered with a scarf to prevent making his girlfriend sick, but they were still very close, like on any other day. It reminded me how love can find a way to conquer all obstacles.

One of my friends told me how meeting a guy with Down Syndrome made her see that people with a disability are a blessing to this world, because they tend to have no sense of prejudice. I'm a big believer in the motto 'Where there's a will, there's a way.'

We build too many walls and not enough bridges. A beautiful story made the worldwide headlines when a mother from Brazil made special assistive equipment so that her son with severe Cerebral Palsy could experience skateboarding. By shining your light on the road ahead, you are helping others see their way too. I will never forget the words from one of my teachers who had kids with autism and specialised in special needs, "I think you're capable of whatever you want."

> *"Pay attention to the things you are naturally drawn to. They are often connected to your path, passion, and purpose in life. Have the courage to follow them."*
>
> Author Unknown

MIRJANA GLIGOREVIC

Resources

Remember to think about what you want to get out of your travels when choosing which company to travel with. Do you want to explore one country thoroughly, or cover a few countries?

Choose a company that aligns with your values. For example, is it eco-friendly? Does it give back to the locals? Is it well suited to your needs?

Intrepid is a good group made up of a relatively small number of people, and they try to leave a positive ecological footprint.

Under30Experiences is a great company for young people who want to focus on one country more deeply, and has a support group for people with a disability called DIVERSEability. It's based in the US, but still gets travellers from all over the world. The founder of the group also has a physical disability, but has climbed Machu Picchu.

How to Choose the Right Travel Company

Base it on:

What type of experience do you want?
E.g., adventurous, historical or cultural?

Find out how they're minimising their global impact. Is it leaving a positive or negative ecological footprint?

Look for less touristy experiences. Big crowds may get in the way of the best sights and potential experiences.

Check how they really feel about animal welfare.

Get as local as possible. Spend time with the locals and embrace their culture, e.g., manners, food.

Find out if they're looking out for women and children. If you want to volunteer with the locals, make sure that your action is benefitting them first.

You can find out how Intrepid Company is catering for people with a 'disability' by visiting:
https://www.intrepidtravel.com/au/accessible-tours-travel

NOTE: Remember to always notify your travel company of your medical needs so they can apply their duty of care and everyone can have the best time.

MIRJANA GLIGOREVIC

If You're Undecided about Travelling with a Carer:

- ❖ Look at the physical rating of the tour.
- ❖ Take into account the most physical aspect of the tour (e.g., climbing).
- ❖ Does it involve uneven or bumpy floor surfaces? You can call and find out from the organisation.
- ❖ Are you independent in your daily life? Are you able to get on and off transport by yourself, carry luggage without help, that sort of thing?
- ❖ If you're not confident in facing those hurdles alone, consider a carer to go on a trip with you.

I recently attended an Assistability expo with services for people with a disability in Australia. They provide many types of support, including in-home support, personal care, education, employment, and travelling support too. You might find a travel buddy through them. For more information, visit:
https://info338547.wixsite.com/website

I also came across a great travel website for people in wheelchairs from one of the empowerment groups on social media. It provides accessibility information on different travel destinations and explains the travel rights of every wheelchair user.
https://ablethrive.com/travel?fbclid=IwAR2_5_IqqzeOOx_F7vNOYFo_uOWxLRrsS9KnrncsHvp5LkiKGMcStms7MvM

For information on all wheelchair accessible places visit:
https://thiis.co.uk/new-google-maps-feature-allows-wheelchair-users-to-discover-wheelchair-accessible-places-globally/

For more specific information about access for travellers with a physical disability from where I went on a tour and beyond, visit:
https://www.sagetraveling.com/

Busabout Company gives you a chance to explore at your own time and pace:
- ❖ Gives you advice on things to do before you get off the bus.
- ❖ The buses come every few days.
- ❖ You meet a new group of people at each stage.

For more information visit:
https://www.busabout.com/

Contiki recently opened up an option for a one-on-one tour. It allows the tour guide to accommodate the individual's particular needs better. For more information visit:
https://www.contiki.com/au/en?fbclid=IwAR0a_AJAFzzqT UYhSMJiN9ipS8q7IS7E6PP143pkcXC5D57GAoE3-TuECAg

Extra Travel Safety Tips:

- ❖ Carry a money belt (a pouch around the waist which goes under your t-shirt).
- ❖ If you don't have a money belt, go to the bathroom when you need to take out your wallet or count the money.
- ❖ Put your backpack at the front of your body or wheelchair instead of at the back.
- ❖ Don't sign any petitions in other countries.

Invisible Disability

The Sunflower Scheme started at airports to make travelling with hidden disabilities, including asthma, autism, depression, epilepsy, fibromyalgia and more, a little easier.

If you are going to the airport and have a hidden disability, please inform the staff prior to travelling as they can arrange a lanyard for you. You can pick it up from the customer service desk upon arrival at the airport or receive it by mail. There are several places you can get the lanyard and use it. They are available from many supermarkets, airports, etc.

These might not be available at all airports just yet, but the good thing is that the world is starting to adjust more for people with special needs. We could also consider making a push to have them available at more airports.

Airport staff can help passengers with lanyards by:
- Giving you more time to prepare for security checks and boarding.
- Letting you stay with family members at all times.
- Giving you clear instructions to follow.
- Explaining what you can expect when travelling through the airport.
- Staff will discreetly come over to anyone who might need additional support at the start and make more way for them.

For more information about the lanyard scheme, please contact a travel agent who can advise you, or contact an airport for more information. Also, most airports will have information about the lanyards, along with support and advice for all disabilities, on their websites, so it might be an idea to check there first.

One mum of twins with ASD in Melbourne has started her own little business in making similar cards for people with some conditions. The ID card describes how the condition affects the person and is a useful tool in helping people find their way when they get lost. You can find North Star Tags on Facebook.

Tip for Parents/Carers of Travellers with Autism:

- Purchase Bose Headphones. They're pricey online but do a great job at blocking out sensory noise and will pay off.
- Try walking on natural surfaces such as grass or sand to help beat jetlag.
- To find out how the world is changing for people with autism visit:

http://edition.cnn.com/travel/article/travellers-with autism/index.html?fbclid=IwAR2TO26oXsdwv3IK3mZbe_fP1AkFFiYiW5k3HTaVcbs8VbdrCV4QgOwAbF8

Acknowledgements

Firstly, I'd like to acknowledge my parents, who have worked very hard and given up much over many years to make me the independent person I am today. Although I was under your wings for a very long time, thank you for bravely putting your feelings aside by deciding to let me go solo to the other end of the world.

Equally, I'd like to acknowledge Baba Stoya and my cousins, Maya and Jenny, for a very warm welcome into their homes, letting me include photos and ensuring that I got the most out of my experience, especially in Belgrade. I'd also like to thank my friend Daria for taking her time to come and meet with me.

I also recognize Travis (my general English tour guide) for helping me overcome some physical barriers by lending me a hand in activities which required balance and coordination support during my tour, as well as my other tour mates. I'm very grateful to have come across some lovely locals including Jovana (Mostar tour guide who also helped me get over the bridge) and my tour mate Eddie, who took a lot of great photos for me.

Many landscape photos without me in this book came from a wide scale of ethnicities/people from all over the Balkans. Their proud permission has also highlighted how the people from different Balkan communities choose kindness for one another in times of need, despite their differences.

Image Acknowledgements: Ana Urošević, Jelena Šćekić, Karmela Marinčić, Ismet Islamović, Antonio Antonovski, Reddit, Orazio Fotti, Iina Kansonen, Rehema Miriam, Croatia

Traveller, Ivona Antich, Roni Jackson- Kerr, Natalia & Jedrzej, Sean Peacock, Ej Wu, Jovana Fuštić, Travelive, Shutterstock, Jeff Hartzog, Duje Radović, thebosnianaussie, Ariana Kajić, EJ Wu and Mitar Milaković.

A special thanks to my book formatter Jan Marshall, who devoted more time than anyone in helping me produce this hard-copy book. She has helped me gain great future skills and I couldn't have done it without her.

I also thank all the other people involved in the best book production, including my editor, Karen Collyer, and cover artist Muqqarib Hassan.

Last, but not least, thank you to all my friends, who always have my back in one way or another.

Thank you for purchasing this book, I hope you got something great out of it. Xx

MIRJANA GLIGOREVIC

About the Author

Mirjana (pronounced Mir-yana) Gligorevic was born with cerebral palsy, but has not let this, or her autism, detract from living a meaningful life. Mirjana didn't have many friends growing-up, but most people know her as a very caring person. She believes her experiences have shaped her into the empath she is today.

Being diagnosed with ASD at age fifteen was a big relief to her, and that's when she really started using the tools to reach her full potential.

Mirjana is inquisitive, outspoken and likes gaining knowledge on different subjects. Although she has found fitting in to everyday society difficult, she has found herself by travelling to different parts of the world.

Her love of travel, sense of accomplishment and adventure has triumphed many things in life. Since finishing Certificate IV in tourism, Mirjana has become a regular volunteer in her op-shop community. Her tasks were quality control of secondhand items such as clothes and toys, and putting them out from time to time. Soon after releasing this book, Mirjana began customer service training in her op-shop, a great experience for her and a big step forward in bringing out her full potential. In 2021, she has found a job as a designated gymnastics coach for little kids on the spectrum and fulfilling her purpose to continue to help people in similar circumstances.

Mirjana has moved out of her parents home prior to releasing this book and describes herself as a very independent woman today. She also hopes to find the man of her dreams and settle in with him.

Facebook:
https://www.facebook.com/MGs-Adventure-Stories-105987178148742/

Instagram:
https://www.instagram.com/mirjanagligorevic/

www.ingramcontent.com/pod-product-compliance
Lightning Source LLC
Chambersburg PA
CBHW070251010526
44107CB00056B/2421